Physical Characteris[tics]
Neapolitan Ma[stiff]
(from The Kennel Club bre[ed])

Body: Longer than height at withers. Broad, well muscled chest, ribcage reaching at least to elbow. Ribs long and well sprung. Topline straight, slightly lower than withers, line of belly parallel to topline.

Tail: Thick at root, set on slightly lower than topline. Tapering towards tip. Customarily docked by one-third length. Never carried up or over back, but may be carried level with topline when moving.

Coat: Short, dense, even, fine, hard texture, with good sheen. No fringe.

Hindquarters: Broad loin, well let into backline, slightly rounded with well developed muscle. Croup broad muscular, with slight slope. Thighs long, broad, moderate stifle, powerful hocks. Dewclaws (single or double) removed.

Colour: Preferred black, blue, all shades of grey, brown varying from fawn to red. Brindling on either of the latter colours. Small star on chest and white on toes permissible. Pigmentation to tone with coat colours.

Size: Height: 65–75 cms (26–29 ins); Weight: 50–70 kgs (110–154 lbs). Some tolerance allowed. Bitches somewhat less.

Feet: Oval; close, arched toes. Pads thick, hard and dark coloured. Nails curved, strong and dark. Hindfeet slightly smaller than front.

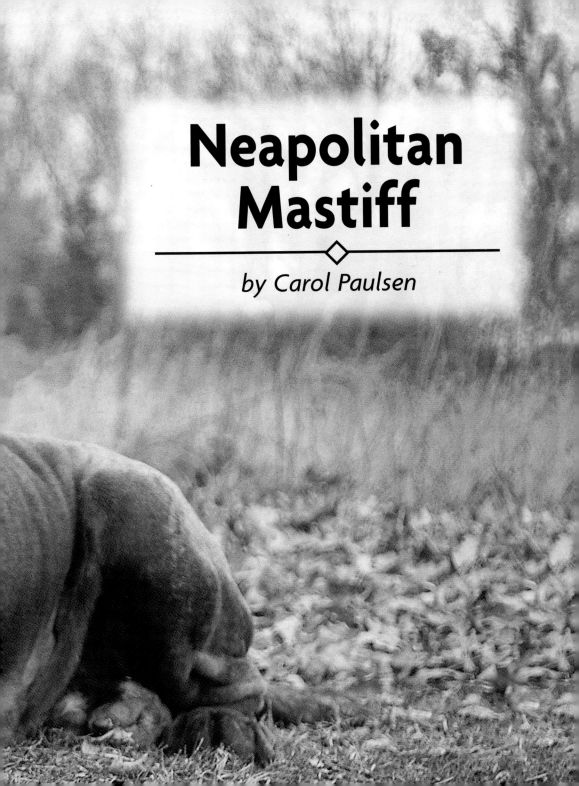

Neapolitan Mastiff

by Carol Paulsen

Table of Contents

Developed from hunters and war dogs, and prized for its unique physical characteristics, the Neapolitan Mastiff's real history begins in the Vesuvius region of Italy. Follow the breed from its beginnings as a valued guard dog to its introduction into countries around the world.

Be advised about choosing a reputable breeder and selecting a healthy, typical puppy. Understand the responsibilities of ownership, including home preparation, acclimatisation, the vet and prevention of common puppy problems.

Learn the requirements of a well-bred Neapolitan Mastiff by studying the description of the breed set forth in The Kennel Club standard. Both show dogs and pets must possess key characteristics as outlined in the breed standard.

PUBLISHED IN THE UNITED KINGDOM BY:

INTERPET
PUBLISHING

Vincent Lane, Dorking
Surrey RH4 3YX
England

ISBN 1-902389-21-2

The Neapolitan Mastiff is one of the world's most distinct breeds in both looks and personality; learn more about his unique characteristics and find out what makes an ideal Neo owner. Also discussed are breed-specific health considerations of which every new owner should be aware.

Enter into a sensible discussion of dietary and feeding considerations, exercise, grooming, travelling and identification of your dog. This chapter discusses Neapolitan Mastiff care for all stages of development.

80
Housebreaking and Training Your Neapolitan Mastiff

by Charlotte Schwartz
Be informed about the importance of training your Neapolitan Mastiff from the basics of housebreaking and understanding the development of a young dog to executing obedience commands (sit, stay, down, etc.).

144
Understanding The Behaviour of Your Neapolitan Mastiff

Learn to recognise and handle common behavioural problems in your Neo, including aggression with people and other dogs, chewing, barking, mounting, digging, jumping up, etc.

PHOTO CREDITS

Norvia Behling
Carolina Biological Supply
Doskocil
Isabelle Francais
James Hayden-Yoav
James R. Hayden, RBP
Carol Ann Johnson
Alice van Kempen
Dwight R Kuhn

Dr Dennis Kunkel
Mikki Pet Products
Carol Paulsen/La Tutela Kennels
Dr Robert L Peiffer, Jr
Phototake
Jean Claude Revy
Dr Andrew Spielman
C James Webb

Illustrations by Renée Low
Special thanks to the owners/breeders of dogs featured in this book: Stan Brown, Philippe Hardy, Carol Paulsen/La Tutela Kennels , Gonnie Schaffer, K Shmuely, G Siano/della Grotta Azzurra and George Small

138
Showing Your Neapolitan Mastiff

Experience the dog show world, including different types of shows and the making up of a champion. Go beyond the conformation ring to working trials and agility trials, etc.

104
Health Care of Your Neapolitan Mastiff

Discover how to select a proper veterinary surgeon and care for your dog at all stages of life. Topics include vaccination scheduling, skin problems, dealing with external and internal parasites and the eye conditions affecting purebred dogs.

Large dogs like the Neapolitan Mastiff have been used as guard and war dogs for thousands of years. Julius Caesar met them during the first century BC when he invaded the British Isles.

HISTORY OF THE
NEAPOLITAN MASTIFF

Both the Metropolitan Museum of Art in New York and the Chicago Art Museum house Mesopotamian terracotta artefacts in the likeness of dogs very similar to the modern Neapolitan Mastiff. An extremely large-headed sitting dog with folds of skin, a powerful muzzle and jaws and amputated ears is depicted in the first, and the second shows a female with the same head type and strength, nursing four puppies. An Assyrian terracotta artefact dating back to the 9th century BC resides in a British museum. Master and dog are depicted, with the master holding the dog by its collar. The dog is pictured with natural ears set rather high on the skull, a massive head with many wrinkles, great dewlap reaching from the mouth to mid-neck and a powerfully built rectangular body set on thick legs. The dog's withers reach the master's belt, indicating his massive size.

Let us begin the history with the Sumerians, who bred large and powerful dogs that were used in battle and to hunt lions and other game. The main characteristics of these dogs were their short, strong muzzles, huge and powerful heads, muscular legs, heavy bone and massive body coupled with great height. These dogs must be considered to be the descendants of the ancient Tibetan Mastiff, who authorities say is the forerunner of all molosser-type dogs. As the Sumerians travelled, they brought their dogs to Mesopotamia 2000 years before the birth of Christ. These mollosers were bred and used to protect property and also to protect livestock from lions. Spreading north, south and east, these dogs eventually reached the Phoenicians. Alexander the Great had many molossians and made a gift of several of these dogs to be taken back to Rome.

During the first century BC, Julius Caesar met with dogs of huge stature and ferocity that he called *Pugnaces Brittaniae* during his campaign in the British Isles. He was so taken with these animals that he took several back to Rome. The presence of these dogs in the British Isles gives credence to the fact that the Phoenicians spread these dogs to the Mediterranean area and points west.

In Roman times the dogs were used as weapons of war and in the circus where they fought wild animals. Handlers and mastiffs fought other handlers and mastiffs in the great coliseums. Roman villas were protected by the mastiffs. After the fall of the Roman Empire, countries were formed and the descendants of these dogs took on the names and the attributes of the countries in which they resided. The dogs that remained in the region near Vesuvius formed a bond with the land and the people. In the days of the Renaissance the mastiff was used as a hunter of large game and as a guard dog.

Latin author Columella, in the first century AD, wrote in his work *De Re Rustica* about the Roman mastiff that was the guardian of the house at that time, '…because a dark dog has a more terrifying appearance; and during the day, a prowler can see him and be frightened by his appearance. When night falls, the dog, lost in the shadows, can attack without being seen. The head is so massive that it seems to be the most important part of the body. The ears fall toward the front, the brilliant and penetrating eyes are black or grey, the chest is deep and hairy, the shoulder wide, the legs thick, the tail short, the hind legs powerful, the toenails strong and great. His temperament must be neither too gentle nor too ferocious and cruel; whereas the first would make him too apt to welcome a thief, the second would predispose him to attack the people of the house.' These words, although written some 2000 years ago, summarise the current-day Neapolitan Mastiff. Columella goes on to say, 'It does not matter that house guard dogs have heavy bodies and are not swift of foot. They are meant to carry out their work from close quarters and do not need to run far.' Thus molossians were bred

Did You Know?

Dogs and wolves are members of the genus *Canis*. Wolves are known scientifically as *Canis lupus* while dogs are known as *Canis domesticus*. Dogs and wolves are

known to interbreed. The term canine derives from the Latin derived word *Canis*. The term dog has no scientific basis but has been used for thousands of years. The origin of the word dog has never been authoritatively ascertained.

and kept large and heavy so that they could bring down an animal or a man and not roam from their homes and their duties as guards. It is said that in ancient times masters would cut off their dog's toes and intentionally cripple them for this very same purpose. The Italian molossian remains virtually unchanged from the time of Columella until this day.

The Italian molossian remained hidden in the Italian countryside for centuries, its temperament and uniqueness being preserved. A well-guarded secret, these molossians were bred and kept in the area of Mt Vesuvius. These relics of a time long gone, with no written word to define the bloodlines, were only brought to light during the latter part of the 1940s. In 1949 Piero Scanziani brought forth this very same dog and it was renamed the Mastino Napoletano. Scanziani, along with other dog enthusiasts, took on the monumental task of writing the standard and ascertaining which of these dogs should be used for breeding. Individuals were visited and measured and their findings recorded. Finally, with written standard in hand, the Mastino Napoletano became a recognised breed with the Italian Kennel Club.

At one point there arose a debate as to the chosen name of our magnificent breed. Some of the breed founders opted for the Molosso Romano as a tribute to Roman Molossian; others wanted the breed name to be Mastino Napoletano, honouring the people and the area that kept this breed alive for centuries. Mastino Napoletano became the breed name of choice though, in my estimation, I feel that Molosso Romano best describes this dog that survived for so many thousands of years.

Some breeding took place between 1949 and 1960. Breed type was set but was somewhat different from that of today's dogs. Less wrinkled and tighter skinned, the breed began its evolution. The 1970s saw many of the greatest dogs come forth. Dogs like Ch Sansone I di Ponzano, Ch Leone, Ch Socrates di Ponzano, Ch Madigam della Grotta Azzurra and Falco della Grotta Azzurra, just to name a few, imprinted their type upon the breed not only in Italy but also in France and other European countries. In the late 1970s 16 outstanding individuals were imported into Germany where, for some unknown reason, the breeding ceased. These 16

The Italian Kennel Club was first to recognise the Neapolitan Mastiff, or Mastino Napoletano.

The Tibetan Mastiff is an Asian guard/war dog. Authorities believe that this breed is the forerunner of all molosser-type dogs.

The Cane Corso is another Italian breed, also part of the mastiff family.

Mastini consisted of 10 dogs and 6 bitches. The dogs that were imported from northern Italy were Int Ch Enea di Ponzano and Int/Ital Ch Aronne. The remaining eight who came from southern Italy were Ital Ch Mason della Grotta Azzurra, Attila della Grotta Azzurra, Unno, Sarno, Oro, Ur, Nerone and Ital Ch Califf della Dea Partenopea. The bitches Teresina della Casa Lazzarone and Int Ch Gilda di Ponzano hailed from the South of Italy while the remaining four—Bundessiegerin Romana della Grotta Azzurra, Europasiegerin Medea della Grotta Azzurra, Valeria della Grotta Azzurra and Europasiegerin Pacchiana—were previously from the North. Very few dogs came out

of these excellent specimens; in fact, only Enea was used to any extent in a breeding program. To this day it remains a mystery, although some believe that this mass importation caused a divided camp. Four Germans undertook this importation to improve the breeding of the Mastino in Germany while another small faction did everything in its power to prevent this project from becoming a success, obviously succeeding.

Italian immigrants brought some Neapolitans over to the United States in the early 1900s but the major importer and primary founder of the breed here was Michael Sottile, Sr, president and founder of the NMCA (Neapolitan Mastiff Club of America) in the 1970s. Michael's grandfather, it is said, smuggled four puppies into the United

States in 1902. Along with Michael Sr, Jane Pampalone and Joan (Moran) White played important roles in promoting the breed through dog shows and helped the breed gain popularity. In the 1980s breeding stock and puppies were exported from Italy to foreign countries, including the United States. The shores of America saw the offspring of some magnificent dogs such as El Gavilan dell'Altafiumara, Mosé, Squarcione, Zimbo della Zacchera and Hatrim and Frazier della Grotta Azzurra, just to mention a few.

All of Europe, including Belgium, Hungary, the Netherlands and Yugoslavia, saw importation into their homelands, where excellent dogs are still being produced today. Within the past ten years or so, a heightened awareness of the breed has arisen in both Australia and England.

The Mastiff is one of the more well-known representatives of the breeds whose names include the term 'mastiff.'

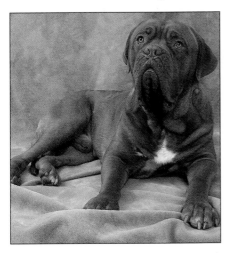

Did You Know?

Since dogs have been inbred for centuries, their physical and mental characteristics are constantly being changed to suit man's desires for hunting, retrieving, scenting, guarding and warming their master's laps. During the past 150 years, dogs have been judged according to physical characteristics as well as functional abilities. Few breeds can boast a genuine balance between physique, working ability and temperament.

The Dogue de Bordeaux is a rare mastiff breed that is becoming quite popular, especially in southern Europe.

13

An adult Neo with natural ears; the puppy's ears have been cropped.

Vera della Grotta Azzurra at two months of age. She is a blue bitch owned by La Tutela Kennels.

Long quarantines in these countries make it quite cost-prohibitive to import puppies and older breeding stock, but there are determined breeders making their mark.

The Neapolitan is experiencing great popularity in the United States at the present time and we are finding more dogs needing rehoming from shelters and unsuitable homes. This is the price a breed pays for notoriety.

Mastinari is the Italian word used for the true Neapolitan Mastiff breeder, a connoisseur and a true artist of the breed, whose blood, sweat and tears have culminated in breeding and producing Mastini that can be considered magnificent creations. This term is not applied to any newcomer to the breed nor ever applied 'lightly' to just any individual breeder. The ideal Neapolitan Mastiff is the true *Mastinari*'s mission and goal. We must pay homage to them for preserving our ancient and noble breed.

15

NEAPOLITAN MASTIFF

PHYSICAL CHARACTERISTICS

The following excerpt is taken from the 1971 FCI Standard on the Neapolitan Mastiff describing the general appearance, conformation, balance and disposition: 'The Neapolitan Mastiff is a guard dog and defence dog par excellence, of great size, powerful and strongly built, of tough yet majestic appearance, sturdy and courageous, of intelligent expression, endowed with correct mental balance and docile character, non-aggressive, indefatigable defender of persons and property. The general conformation is that of a heavy brachymorph, whose trunk is longer than the height at the withers, harmonious as regards size (heterometry) and profile (alloidism). Skin is not adhering to the underlying tissue but abundant, with slack connective tissue over all parts of the body and especially on the head where it forms wrinkles and folds and at the neck where it forms the dewlap.' A better description of this majestic beast can never be found.

Massive is a word which best describes the Neapolitan Mastiff. A large and powerful dog with a brachycephalic and massive skull, wrinkled head, huge bone and stocky body, the typical Neapolitan male weighs in at 60–70 kgs and stands 65–75 cms at the withers. Females are somewhat smaller in size typically 50–60 kgs. The Neapolitan is certainly not the tallest of dogs but next to his English Mastiff cousin, the Neapolitan more often than not appears to be more broad and massive though lighter. Adult height is usually reached at about one year of age, though some individuals may grow an inch or

Why are people drawn to the Neapolitan Mastiff? The breed's unique look, guarding ability and even temperament are several of the many reasons.

Neos take a long time to mature, often not reaching their adult weight until over three years of age.

so more after that. Adult weight is generally not reached until the dog is three to three-and-a-half years of age and sometimes older. Like all giant breeds, the Neapolitan is slow to mature and his puppyhood is long. He is not considered to be a mature specimen until the age of three. Unfortunately, this wonderful animal, like all other giant breeds, does not have a long life. The Neapolitan's life span is eight to ten years.

Having a short, stiff, hard and dense coat of uniform length and smoothness all over the body, the Neapolitan Mastiff is virtually a wash-and-wear dog. No extensive grooming is required except during the two shedding periods, spring and fall. I find that a shedding blade coupled with a mitt of sisal or horsehair will help remove all dead hair. The accepted coat colours are black, blue (all shades of grey), tawny and mahogany, all with or without brindling (a slight striping on all or part of the coat). In the Neapolitan, brindling is not a colour but a marking. White markings are acceptable on tips of toes and on the chest. All puppies are born with blue eyes that change to correspond to the coat colour at three to four months of age. In black dogs the eyes are usually brown; hazel is common in the blue specimens. The natural ear of the Neapolitan is small in relation to the size of the dog. It is triangular in shape, set above the zygomatic arch (cheekbone) and lying flat and close to the cheek. Traditionally cropped, they form an equilateral triangle. Cropping of the ear is not required for the show ring;

Neapolitans may be shown with natural ears or cropped ears. The cropped ear gives the dog a more alert expression. The tail is always docked to two-thirds of its original length, reaching or slightly exceeding the top of the hock. The tail should be broad and thick at the root, tapering slightly at the tip and set slightly lower than the dog's topline.

Neos are born with drop ears, yet many owners choose to have their dogs' ears cropped to give a more alert expression.

PERSONALITY

The Neapolitan Mastiff is a loyal, peaceful and steady dog, not aggressive or prone to biting without reason. A superior guardian of his persons and property, the Neapolitan is a vigilant, intelligent, noble and majestic beast. It is not uncommon for the Neapolitan to be stubborn, headstrong, independent and strong-willed, and sometimes shy; however, shy dogs should never be bred. Wary of strangers but a wonderful, loving companion with his own family, the Neapolitan needs socialisation to become accustomed to different people, places and things. Most Neapolitans prefer to be homebodies and are not advocates of change. Social interaction with people is a must and the Neapolitan should be taken off the premises, touched and petted by as many people as possible when still a puppy. When the interaction is positive, the Neapolitan should be showered with praise. Most owners are concerned that high levels of socialisation will diminish the Neapolitan's ability to be a guard dog and protect his home and family, but nothing could be further from the truth. This trait has been bred into the breed for centuries; it is not changed that easily. It is imperative, though, that an owner of a Neapolitan never forget the dog's strong, natural and primitive

The female Neo, shown here, is typically smaller than the male, weighing on average about 10 kgs less.

instincts. The Neapolitan Mastiff owner, in order to raise a good canine citizen, must always be aware of the thoughts and behaviour of dogs, and must couple this awareness with responsible, consistent discipline.

Because of the love the Neapolitan has for his home and family, he will not stray—a wanderer he is not. His master is everything to the Neapolitan; he would rather be with his master than do anything else. He seeks the companionship of his master more so than that of another dog or animal. Your Neapolitan will follow you from room to room and lie at your feet waiting for your next move. His master is his world. This being said, it is no surprise that the Neapolitan Mastiff is loyal to a fault. A few kind words and loving touches will endear you to him forever.

19

Neapolitans by nature are dominant alpha dogs and must be handled accordingly. It is important to remember that every member of the family, including the children, must outrank the Neapolitan in pack member status. Please be aware that the Neapolitan is an adult's dog, not a dog meant for children's entertainment. If you are looking for a dog for your children to be their nursemaid and to roughhouse with, then consider another breed. As a rule, no dog, large or small, should be left with children unattended. This is an accident waiting to happen; if you are unable to supervise your dog around children, please separate the dog from them. All activity, including play, between the Neapolitan and the children should be done in the presence of at least one adult. Most Neapolitans are fond of their human children and would not purposely hurt them, but, because of their large size, they could knock over a small child and step on him in their exuberance. The Neapolitan deserves and commands respect from adults and children alike.

Neapolitans are generally

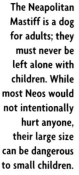

The Neapolitan Mastiff is a dog for adults; they must never be left alone with children. While most Neos would not intentionally hurt anyone, their large size can be dangerous to small children.

tolerant of other animals but it is not recommended that the Neapolitan share the household with another dog with an alpha nature. If two Neapolitans of the same sex are housed together, they may have to be separated as the severity of their disagreements increases. When a female is kept with a male Neapolitan, she usually takes charge if the male allows himself to become subservient. I have seen males and females fight for the alpha position in the pack. I recommend, from my own personal experiences, that each dog, male and female, be housed separately when left alone to

The Neo is a giant dog. This is not a breed to be carried around; as they grow, it doesn't take long before they become too heavy to lift.

Dogs, Dogs, Good for Your Heart!

People usually purchase dogs for companionship, but studies show that dogs can help to improve their owners' health and level of activity, as well as lower a human's risk of coronary heart disease. Without even realising it, when a person puts time into exercising, grooming and feeding a dog, he also puts more time into his own personal health care. Dog owners establish a more routine schedule for their dogs to follow, which can have positive effects on a human's health. Dogs also teach us patience, offer unconditional love and provide the joy of having a furry friend to pet!

prevent fighting and bloodshed. It truly is not worthwhile having your prized possession maimed or disfigured because you are seeking the 'Peaceable Kingdom.'

Loving the chase, the Neapolitan will often pursue a runner or bicyclist, and most have been known to chase cats or quick-moving animals like rabbits. This is why it is important that the Neapolitan be obedience trained and his energy channelled properly. All dogs must be taught what is acceptable and unacceptable behaviour; therefore, obedience training for the Neapolitan is a must. Consistency is the key. With a dog the size of the

21

Neapolitan it is imperative that the owner be in charge at all times. The owner has this obligation to himself, to his dog and to others.

Neapolitans love to chew; adequate toys and various non-harmful types of bones should help to alleviate this problem. However, until he can be safely left in the home without causing destruction, it is recommended that crate training be employed.

It should be noted that the Neapolitan is the messiest of eaters. His copious flews and large lips scatter food in all directions and are great hiding places for snacks long after the meal is over. Neapolitans need significant quantities of both food and water, and with drinking and eating comes the drool. All Neapolitans drool to some extent. Their drool is a heavy, thick saliva with the consistency of egg whites. Most Neapolitans do not drool all the time, although I have had some, three males in particular come to mind, that seemed as if their mouths were perpetual faucets. Drooling can and does also occur during periods of nervousness and hot weather conditions.

Another endearing habit of the Neapolitan, as is true with all mastiff-type dogs, is snoring. A sound-asleep Neapolitan resting contentedly on the second floor of a house can be heard on the first floor right through the floorboards! This certainly does not sit well with humans who tend to be light sleepers.

The Neapolitan is not a suitable dog for everyone. It is definitely not for the first-time dog owner, and the prospective owner should have some experience with dominant alpha dogs. The Neapolitan cannot be expected to spend its entire life isolated in a backyard with only food and water and no attention or socialisation. Neapolitans need attention, discipline and human companionship. A

Neapolitan is a large, vocal and messy animal, so in all fairness to the dog, please research the breed carefully.

Neapolitan Mastiffs are not particularly active or fast-moving dogs. Their large, heavy size prevents them from moving too quickly.

WORKING DOG OR HOME COMPANION?

The Neapolitan Mastiff is a natural guard. To try to separate the companion dog from the working dog in this breed is an impossible task. They are always on guard—this is their job—and they will do it while being your companion. The Neapolitan takes his job as a working dog seriously. His fierce appearance and gargoyle-like head add to his being a deterrent to home intrusion. Although appearing slow and lumbering, the Neapolitan can become aroused in a moment to protect his property or his charges. However, on the whole, the Neapolitan is an even-tempered animal who loves to cuddle up on the couch and sleep, reserving his energy for times when it is needed. He is not a patrolling dog by nature; he watches and waits and strikes when necessary.

VERSATILITY AND AGILITY

The role of the Neapolitan is that of a guardian. This is what he was bred for and he does his job well.

We have since broadened the horizons for this majestic breed opening up new and different challenges for our Mastini. In obedience work Neapolitans seem to do well in a class setting, but in formal obedience trials they are not the quick-responding dog that the Shepherds, Aussies, Goldens or Shelties are. They are generally slow moving and contemplative, almost mulling over the commands before acting on them. Obedience judges are just starting to recognise this, and more mastiff dogs are receiving higher obedience scores.

The Neapolitan is not the best selection of a dog for athletic ability and endurance. Yes, there are some that excel, but they are the exceptions. Running alongside a bike and jogging is not the Neapolitan's forte. They are heavy for their height and their stamina is not the greatest; they fatigue and overheat easily. Most Neapolitan Mastiffs love to swim and this is a good form of exercise for them since it is gentle on their joints and limbs. Puppies should never be heavily exercised, as this will result in damage to the joints and ligaments that will cause skeletal damage as they grow. Short walks for a small puppy are fine and stair climbing should be limited. The Neapolitan has a very high tolerance for pain and, because of this, injuries can go unnoticed and untreated.

HEALTH CONSIDERATIONS AND HEREDITARY DISEASES
One of the unique features of the Neapolitan is its loose skin and wrinkles. Despite what one would think from his appearance, the Neapolitan generally does not suffer from skin problems. The dog should be kept clean and parasite-free and there should be no skin problems.

Demodecosis (demodectic mange) generally runs in certain lines, and dogs suffering from weak immune systems displaying this disease should be spayed or neutered and not bred. The mites, which inhabit all

dogs, multiply in such abundant numbers that they cause hair to fall out, pustules to form and infection to set in. This is usually seen in puppies but it has been known to appear in females during oestrus and some males reaching puberty. Your veterinary surgeon can recommend the appropriate topical solution and/or oral antibiotics for the irritation.

Emotionally and economically, the *Demodex* mite reeks havoc on both the Neapolitan Mastiff and his owner, but once

treatment is complete all is back to normal. Be aware that this condition is hereditary and that breeding animals that have been prone to *Demodex* and that have poor immune systems can and does add to the canine population's suffering from skin disorders.

Cherry eye is a problem in the Neapolitan but is not unique to this breed. It is simply the prolapse of the gland of the third eyelid. The loose connective tissue of the Neapolitan contributes to this ailment. This unsightly red and swollen gland can be removed under anaesthesia by snipping it out. Some veterinary surgeons advocate tacking the gland back down under the third eyelid, but this procedure has never been seen to work successfully in the Neapolitan. Contrary to popular belief, removal of the gland, if done correctly, will not cause 'dry eye' or reoccurrence. The third eyelid must be left intact.

Canine hip dysplasia and elbow dysplasia are also seen in the Neapolitan Mastiff. Complex in nature, these two conditions are fairly common in large and small breeds alike. The Neapolitan has loose joints and connective tissue, but joint laxity does not equate to hip dysplasia. At present, there are many prescription medications and over-the-counter medications to alleviate the symptoms of hip dysplasia. There are also various surgical procedures to correct the problem. These options should be discussed with your veterinary surgeon on a case-by-case basis. Suffice it to say that only sound, beautiful specimens should be bred.

Ruptured anterior cruciate ligament, 'football injury,' occurs when the dog suffers trauma to the stifle. This can happen while running and turning improperly on the back legs, tearing the ligament that holds the knee

The Neapolitan Mastiff is constantly on guard; it is his job by instinct. Having this Neo watching over your garden means that your home is well protected.

Large breeds are prone to the crippling condition known as hip dysplasia. This is a condition of the hip joints, in which the bones do not fit into the hip sockets properly.

together. A competent orthopaedic surgeon should be sought out for the surgery. Rest and no stair climbing are recommended after the procedure.

Panosteitis (or wandering lameness or growing pains) usually appears in puppies 4 to 18 months of age and usually subsides as the dog reaches the age of two. Symptoms are limping, pain travelling from leg to leg and difficulty in jumping and getting up. Rest is the treatment recommended along with some anti-inflammatory medications.

Entropion (turning in of the eyelid) and ectropion (turning out of the eyelid) are seen in some specimens. This too can be surgically corrected if it is not outgrown in puppies.

The Neapolitan tolerates cold weather better than he does the heat. Thus, it is quite easy for a Neapolitan to suffer overheating and stroke. Water and shade should always be made available to outside dogs.

Hosing them down will help to keep them cool during the hot summer weather. Many a Neapolitan has died because his owner did not provide proper conditions for his survival in hot and humid temperatures.

Even though short-haired, the Neapolitan can easily tolerate freezing, even below-freezing, winter weather as long as he has shelter from the cold and the elements. Bedding can, and should, consist of straw, as straw provides warmth and comfort and is not easily broken down.

Another issue of concern in the Neapolitan Mastiff is the breed's low tolerance for anaesthesia and tranquillisers. Many a Neapolitan has died on the operating table because of an overdose of anaesthesia. The veterinary surgeon should be made aware of this prior to surgery. Tranquillisers also should be given with a light hand. Dosage can always be increased, but once ingested it can be difficult and nearly impossible to reverse.

DO YOU KNOW ABOUT HIP DYSPLASIA?

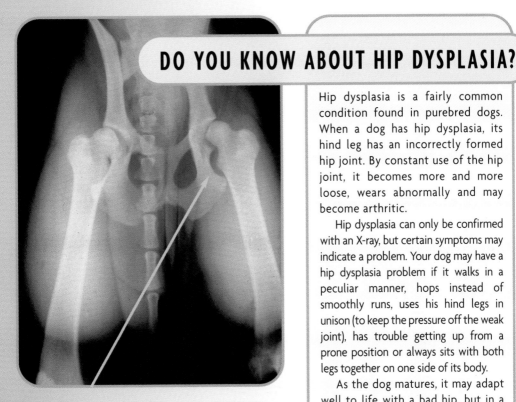

Hip dysplasia is a fairly common condition found in purebred dogs. When a dog has hip dysplasia, its hind leg has an incorrectly formed hip joint. By constant use of the hip joint, it becomes more and more loose, wears abnormally and may become arthritic.

Hip dysplasia can only be confirmed with an X-ray, but certain symptoms may indicate a problem. Your dog may have a hip dysplasia problem if it walks in a peculiar manner, hops instead of smoothly runs, uses his hind legs in unison (to keep the pressure off the weak joint), has trouble getting up from a prone position or always sits with both legs together on one side of its body.

As the dog matures, it may adapt well to life with a bad hip, but in a few years the arthritis develops and many dogs with hip dysplasia become cripples.

Hip dysplasia is considered an inherited disease and can only be diagnosed definitely when the dog is two years old. Some experts claim that a special diet might help your puppy outgrow the bad hip, but the usual treatments are surgical. The removal of the pectineus muscle, the removal of the round part of the femur, reconstructing the pelvis and replacing the hip with an artificial one are all surgical interventions that are expensive, but they are usually very successful. Follow the advice of your veterinary surgeon.

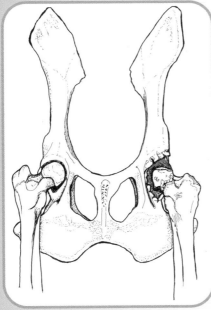

Hip dysplasia is a badly worn hip joint caused by improper fit of the bone into the socket. It is easily the most common hip problem in larger dogs. The illustration shows a healthy hip joint on the left and an unhealthy hip joint on the right.

NEAPOLITAN MASTIFF

The Neapolitan Mastiff is recognised by the Fédération Cynologique Internationale (FCI); The Kennel Club recognises it as an Interim breed, which is a breed that is not yet granted Kennel Club Challenge Certificate status.

THE KENNEL CLUB INTERIM STANDARD FOR THE NEAPOLITAN MASTIFF

General Appearance: Well boned, large, strongly built, vigorous, alert and muscular. Of majestic bearing, with intelligent expression.

Characteristics: A degree of loose-fitting skin over body and head, with some dewlap, is a feature, not to be excessive.

Temperament: Devoted and loyal guard of owner and property.

Head and Skull: Head large, broad short skull. Broad across cheeks. Head proportion: skull length 2:3 to muzzle 1:3. Top of skull parallel to topline of muzzle.

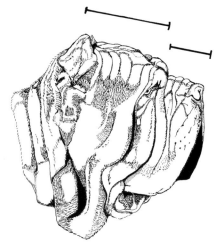

A correct head with the proper proportions.

Well pronounced, definite stop, nose should not protrude beyond vertical line of muzzle. Nose large with well opened nostrils, lips full and heavy. Upper lip resembles inverted V. Muzzle deep, sides flat and vertical, showing flews. Head deep and spherical.

Eyes: Set forward, well apart, rather rounded. Set fairly deep. Rim pigmentation to tone with nose colour.

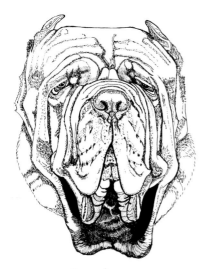

Cropped ears.

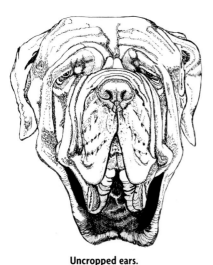

Uncropped ears.

Mouth: Teeth white and regular. Strong, well developed jaws, with scissor bite, but level tolerated. Scissor bite, i.e. upper teeth closely overlapping lower teeth and set square to the jaws.

Neck: Short, stocky, very muscular, dewlap from lower jaw reaching mid-point of neck.

Forequarters: Shoulder long, slightly sloping with well developed and definite muscle. Elbows not too close to body to allow very free action. Pasterns slightly sloping, legs vertical when viewed from front.

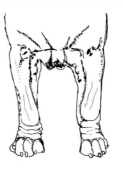 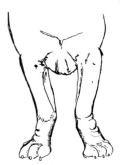

Top left: Correct, straight forelegs.
Top right: Incorrect forelegs, turning out.
Bottom left: Correct, straight hindquarters.
Bottom right: Incorrect, overly angulated, weak hindquarters.

Ears: Small for size of head, set forward, high and well apart. Triangular, hanging flat towards cheeks, but not reaching beyond line of throat.

Top: skin hangs loose in folds; even topline.

Bottom: Insufficient amount of skin (folds); uneven topline.

Body: Longer than height at withers. Broad, well muscled chest, ribcage reaching at least to elbow. Ribs long and well sprung. Topline straight, slightly lower than withers, line of belly parallel to topline.

Hindquarters: Broad loin, well let into backline, slightly rounded with well developed muscle. Croup broad muscular, with slight slope. Thighs long, broad, moderate stifle, powerful hocks. Dewclaws (single or double) removed.

Feet: Oval; close, arched toes. Pads thick, hard and dark coloured. Nails curved, strong and dark. Hindfeet slightly smaller than front.

When a Neo has a sufficient amount of skin, its jowls can be extended as shown.

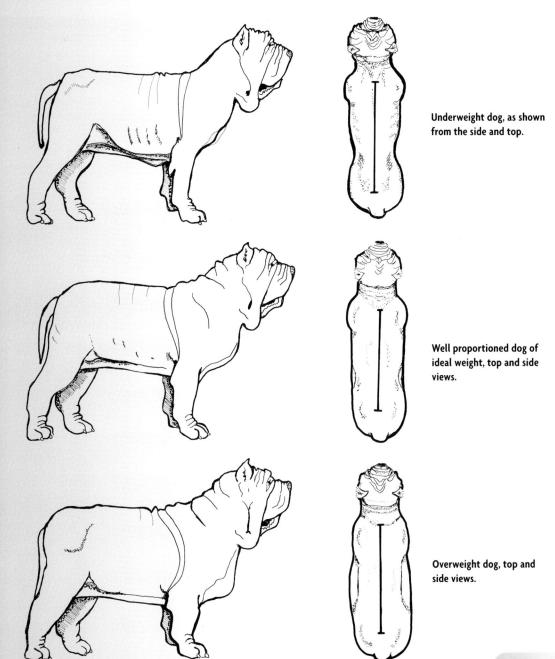

Underweight dog, as shown from the side and top.

Well proportioned dog of ideal weight, top and side views.

Overweight dog, top and side views.

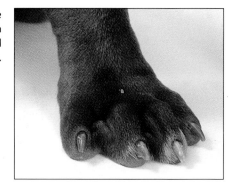

Close-up of the Neo's foot, with nicely trimmed nails.

If you intend to show your Neo, you must make this intention clear to the breeder from the start. An experienced breeder can make an educated prediction as to how well the puppy will eventually conform to the standard.

Tail: Thick at root, set on slightly lower than topline. Tapering towards tip. Customarily docked by one-third length. Never carried up or over back, but may be carried level with topline when moving.

Gait/Movement: Slow, free, bear-like. Slow trot, long steps covering ground well. Rarely gallops.

Coat: Short, dense, even, fine, hard texture, with good sheen. No fringe.

Colour: Preferred black, blue, all shades of grey, brown varying from fawn to red. Brindling on either of the latter colours. Small star on chest and white on toes permissible. Pigmentation to tone with coat colours.

Size: Height: 65–75 cms (26–29 ins); Weight: 50–70 kgs (110–154 lbs). Some

tolerance allowed. Bitches somewhat less.

Faults: Any departure from the foregoing points should be considered a fault and the seriousness with which the fault should be regarded should be in exact proportion to its degree.

Note: Male animals should have two apparently normal testicles fully descended into the scrotum.

The proper gait for the Neo is slow, free and bear-like. Although he does not move quickly, the Neo covers a lot of ground with his long strides.

A very nicely proportioned Neapolitan Mastiff in an alert pose.

NEAPOLITAN MASTIFF

Selecting a purebred dog from a responsible breeder will allow for a higher degree of predictability regarding temperament, health, working ability, size, coat, etc. A responsible breeder cares about each dog he/she brings into the world and will take positive steps to ensure that his/her dogs do not land in a shelter or rescue.

Select your Neo breeder before you select your Neo puppy.

Responsible breeders require deposits before puppies are born to encourage commitment from potential owners. They interview

Did You Know?

Unfortunately, when a puppy is bought by someone who does not take into consideration the time and attention that dog ownership requires, it is the puppy who suffers when he is either abandoned or placed in a shelter by a frustrated owner. So all of the 'homework' you do in preparation for your pup's arrival will benefit you both. The more informed you are, the more you will know what to expect and the better equipped you will be to handle the ups and downs of raising a puppy. Hopefully, everyone in the household is willing to do his part in raising and caring for the pup. The anticipation of owning a dog often brings a lot of promises from excited family members: 'I will walk him every day,' 'I will feed him,' 'I will housebreak him,' etc., but these things take time and effort, and promises can easily be forgotten once the novelty of the new pet has worn off.

Did You Know?

You should not even think about buying a puppy that looks sick, undernourished, overly frightened or nervous. Sometimes a timid puppy will warm up to you after a 30-minute 'let's-get-acquainted' session.

the interested parties and are honest about the qualities of the dogs they have bred. They will always be available to their buyers to answer questions regarding raising, training and caring for the new puppy. A responsible breeder will always take back or help place a dog they have bred.

Responsible breeders know the typical genetic diseases of the breed and do not breed dogs that may pass on genetic problems. They ensure that the dogs they produce are capable of full, healthy, happy lives, sound in mind, body and temperament. Shy and aggressive dogs are never bred by responsible, caring breeders.

A responsible breeder is usually active in dog clubs or shows his/her dogs. Litters are kept to a minimum, usually one to three per year. Responsible breeders are in touch with their puppy buyers, even after a period of years. The breeder should be curious about you, concerned about the welfare of his or her

puppies. The breeder will ask you questions and insist on certain criteria being met before placing a puppy. A good responsible breeder will be willing to discuss all the genetic problems, nutrition, socialisation and training of your puppy with you. He or she should be there for you for the remainder of your puppy's life.

Where possible, the kennel should be visited. The kennel

usually consists of indoor/outdoor runs and exercise yards, or it may be simply the breeder's home. It should be clean and free of excrement, just like the puppies. This goes for all of the dogs in the kennel—they should all be clean and brushed and should have fresh food and water. The runs should be large enough to accommodate the size of the dog contained therein. The dogs should appear healthy, friendly and outgoing towards humans; the health of the older dogs on the

The time you spend getting to know your new puppy will form a bond that lasts a lifetime.

Neapolitan Mastiff

A new puppy means toilet accidents around your home until he is house-broken. Be prepared.

premises will tell you a great deal about the kennel.

Human contact is important, so the first few weeks of a puppy's life should be shared with humans to form the proper bond.

Did You Know?

Your selection of a good puppy can be determined by your needs. A show potential or a good pet? It is your choice. Every puppy, however, should be of good temperament. Although show-quality puppies are bred and raised with emphasis on physical conformation, responsible breeders strive for equally good temperament. Do not buy from a breeder who concentrates solely on physical beauty at the expense of personality.

Puppies should always be raised in the house in constant contact with people, sounds and everyday household events. Puppies should be active and playful, eager to meet people and not shy. There should be no discharge from the eyes, nose or ears, and the gums should be pink and firm. A puppy should be plump, but without a distended belly, and should move around freely without signs of lameness. Pick a puppy that will naturally follow you, is not upset over sudden, loud sounds and has confidence to explore new areas without fear. Your puppy should have had at least one set of shots, preferably two, and should have been dewormed and examined by a veterinary surgeon. Your breeder of choice should provide you with a pedigree, registration papers, test results, pamphlets on puppy care, feeding instructions and maintenance, and a written guarantee covering genetic and congenital problems at the time of puppy purchase. Most of all, trust your common sense and your instincts—if it does not feel right, walk away.

The ideal situation when purchasing a puppy is the ability to see both sire and dam but, when this is not possible, at least the dam should be available for viewing. The dam should be in good condition—healthy, strong, well-fed and possessing the proper look and temperament that

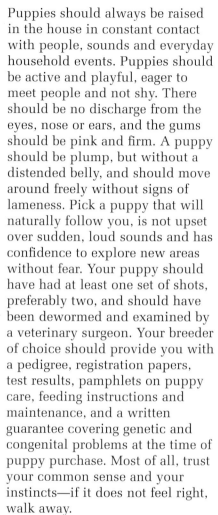

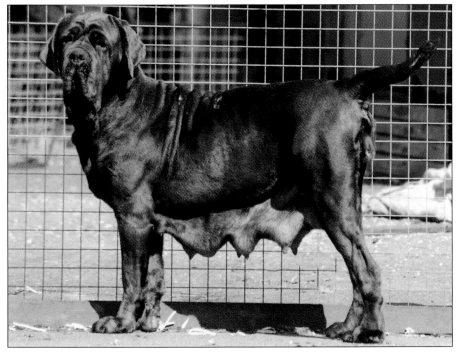

Puppies get a healthy start in life from their mother's milk. A nursing mother is very easy to spot!

would warrant her being bred. The puppies should be available for viewing at eight weeks of age when the immunity provided from their mother's milk has worn off and their vaccinations have taken hold. Ideally at this age, the puppy should have a series of at least two shots. Once the puppy goes home with a new owner, the veterinary surgeon will continue the pup on an appropriate vaccination schedule.

COMMITMENT OF OWNERSHIP
After considering all of these factors, you have most likely already made some very

important decisions about selecting your puppy. You have chosen a Neapolitan Mastiff,

Did You Know?

Your puppy should have a well-fed appearance but not a distended abdomen, which may indicate worms or incorrect feeding, or both. The body should be firm, with a solid feel. The skin of the abdomen should be pale pink and clean, without signs of scratching or rash. Check the hind legs to make certain that dewclaws were removed, if any were present at birth.

37

Your Schedule...

If you lead an erratic, unpredictable life, with daily or weekly changes in your work requirements, consider the problems of owning a puppy. The new puppy has to be fed regularly, socialised (loved, petted, handled, introduced to other people) and, most importantly, allowed to visit outdoors for toilet training. As the dog gets older, it can be more tolerant of deviations in its feeding and toilet relief.

water and shelter, your pup needs care, protection, guidance and love. If you are not prepared to commit to this, then you are not prepared to own a dog.

Wait a minute, you say. How hard could this be? All of my neighbours own dogs and they seem to be doing just fine. Why should I have to worry about all of this? Well, you should not worry about it; in fact, you will probably find that once your Neapolitan Mastiff pup gets used to his new home, he will fall into his place in the family quite naturally. But it never hurts to emphasise the commitment of dog ownership. With some time and patience, it is really not too difficult to raise a curious and exuberant Neapolitan Mastiff pup to be a well-adjusted and well-mannered adult dog—a dog that could be your most loyal friend.

PREPARING PUPPY'S PLACE
Researching your breed and finding a breeder are only two aspects of the 'homework' you will have to do before bringing your Neapolitan Mastiff puppy home. You will also have to prepare your home and family for the new addition. Much as you would prepare a nursery for a new-born baby, you will need to designate a place in your home that will be the puppy's own. How you prepare your home will depend on how much freedom the dog will be allowed. Whatever you decide, you must ensure that he has a place that he can 'call his own.'

When you bring your new puppy into your home, you are bringing him into what will become his home as well. Obviously, you did not buy a puppy so that he could take over your house, but in order for a puppy to grow into a stable, well-adjusted dog, he has to feel comfortable in his surroundings. Remember, he is leaving the warmth and security of his mother and littermates, as well as the familiarity of the only place he has ever known, so it is important to make his transition as easy as possible. By preparing a place in your home for the puppy, you are making him feel as welcome as possible in a strange new place. It should not take him long to get used to it, but the sudden shock of being transplanted is somewhat traumatic for a young pup. Imagine how a small child would feel in the same situation—that is how your puppy must be feeling. It is up to you to reassure him and to let him know, 'Little fellow, you are going to like it here!'

WHAT YOU SHOULD BUY

CRATE

To someone unfamiliar with the use of crates in dog training, it

> **Are You a Fit Owner?**
>
> If the breeder from whom you are buying a puppy asks you a lot of personal questions, do not be insulted. Such a breeder wants to be sure that you will be a fit provider for his puppy.

popular and very successful housebreaking method. A crate can keep your dog safe during travel; and, perhaps most importantly, a crate provides your

may seem like punishment to shut a dog in a crate, but this is not the case at all. Although all breeders do not advocate crate training, more and more breeders and trainers are recommending crates as a preferred tool for pet puppies as well as show puppies. Crates are not cruel—crates have many humane and highly effective uses in dog care and training. For example, crate training is a very

dog with a place of his own in your home. It serves as a 'doggie bedroom' of sorts—your Neapolitan Mastiff can curl up in his crate when he wants to sleep or when he just needs a break. Many dogs sleep in their crates overnight. When lined with soft bedding and with a favourite toy placed inside, a crate becomes a cosy pseudo-den for your dog. Like his ancestors, he too will

A litter of baby Neos, each one equally adorable! Don't let 'puppy cuteness' be the only factor in your choice of a pup; behaviour and temperament are more important.

41

The Neo puppy will grow into a very large dog. This crate is appropriate for the young Neo, but he will outgrow it quickly as he gets older.

Facing page: Your local pet shop should be able to show you a variety of crates in all sizes and price ranges.

seek out the comfort and retreat of a den—you just happen to be providing him with something a little more luxurious than what his early ancestors enjoyed.

As far as purchasing a crate, the type that you buy is up to you. It will most likely be one of the two most popular types: wire or fibreglass. There are advantages and disadvantages to each type. For example, a wire crate is more open, allowing the air to flow through and affording the dog a view of what is going on around him whilst a fibreglass crate is

PHOTO COURTESY OF DOSKOCIL.

Crate Training Tips

During crate training, you should partition off the section of the crate in which the pup stays. If he is given too big an area, this will hinder your training efforts. Crate training is based on the fact that a dog does not like to soil his sleeping quarters, so it is ineffective to keep a pup in a crate that is so big that he can eliminate in one end and get far enough away from it to sleep. Also, you want to make the crate den-like for the pup. Blankets and a favourite toy will make the crate cosy for the small pup; as he grows, you may want to evict some of his 'roommates' to make more room.

It will take some coaxing at first, but be patient. Given some time to get used to it, your pup will adapt to his new home-within-a-home quite nicely.

sturdier. Both can double as travel crates, providing protection for the dog. The size of the crate is another thing to consider. Puppies do not stay puppies forever—in fact, sometimes it seems as if they

43

grow right before your eyes. A
Yorkie-sized crate may be fine for
a very young Neapolitan Mastiff
pup, but it will not do him much
good for long! Unless you have
the money and the inclination to
buy a new crate every time your
pup has a growth spurt, it is better
to get one that will accommodate
your dog both as a pup and at full
size. An extra-large crate will be
necessary for a full-grown
Neapolitan Mastiff, who stands
approximately 26 to 29 inches
high.

BEDDING
Veterinary bedding in the dog's
crate will help the dog feel more
at home and you may also like to

pop in a small blanket. This will
take the place of the leaves, twigs,
etc., that the pup would use in the
wild to make a den; the pup can
make his own 'burrow' in the
crate. Although your pup is far
removed from his den-making
ancestors, the denning instinct is

Your Neo puppy
should have soft
bedding or a
blanket with
which to snuggle.
He needs
something warm
and cuddly to
replace the
warmth of his
mother and
littermates.

Natural Toxins

Examine your grass and garden landscaping before bringing your puppy home. Many varieties of plants have leaves, stems or flowers that are toxic if ingested, and you can depend on a curious puppy to investigate them. Ask your vet for information on poisonous plants or research them at your library.

A very useful device for all dog owners is a 'poop-scoop.' Be a good citizen and clean up after your Neo, even in your own garden.

you go along—grooming supplies, flea/tick protection, baby gates to partition a room, etc. These things will vary depending on your situation but it is important that you have everything you need to feed and make your Neapolitan Mastiff comfortable in his first few days at home.

PUPPY-PROOFING YOUR HOME
Aside from making sure that your Neapolitan Mastiff will be comfortable in your home, you also have to make sure that your home is safe for your Neapolitan Mastiff. This means taking precautions that your pup will not get into anything he should not get into and that there is nothing within his reach that may harm him should he sniff it, chew it, inspect it, etc. This probably seems obvious since, whilst you are primarily concerned with your pup's safety, at the same time you do not want your belongings to be ruined. Breakables should be

placed out of reach if your dog is to have full run of the house. If he is to be limited to certain places within the house, keep any potentially dangerous items in the 'off-limits' areas. An electrical cord can pose a danger should the puppy decide to taste it—and who

Chemical Toxins

Scour your garage for potential puppy dangers. Remove weed killers, pesticides and antifreeze materials. Antifreeze is highly toxic and even a few drops can kill an adult dog. The sweet taste attracts the animal, who will quickly consume it from the floor or curbside.

is going to convince a pup that it would not make a great chew toy? Cords should be fastened tightly against the wall. If your dog is going to spend time in a crate, make sure that there is nothing near his crate that he can reach if he sticks his curious little nose or paws through the openings. Just as you would with a child, keep

Did You Know?

It will take at least two weeks for your puppy to become accustomed to his new surroundings. Give him lots of love, attention, handling, frequent opportunities to relieve himself, a diet he likes to eat and a place he can call his own.

all household cleaners and chemicals where the pup cannot get to them.

It is also important to make sure that the outside of your home is safe. Of course your puppy should never be unsupervised, but a pup let loose in the garden will want to run and explore, and he should be granted that freedom. Do not let a fence give you a false sense of security; you would be surprised how crafty (and persistent) a dog can be in figuring out how to dig under and squeeze his way through small holes, or to jump or climb over a fence. The remedy is to make the fence high enough so that it really is impossible for your dog to get over it (about four metres should suffice), and well embedded into the ground. Be sure to repair or secure any gaps in the fence. Check the fence periodically to ensure that it is in good shape and make repairs as needed; a very determined pup may return to the same spot to 'work on it' until he is able to get through.

Your house is not the only area to puppy-proof; the garden needs to be safe for your pup as well. Make sure that there are no poisonous plants in the garden and that you do not use harmful chemicals on the grass.

Did You Know?

Taking your dog from the breeder to your home in a car can be a very uncomfortable experience for both of you. The puppy will have been taken from his warm, friendly, safe environment and brought into a strange new environment. An environment that moves! Be prepared for loose bowels, urination, crying, whining and even fear biting. With proper love and encouragement when you arrive home, the stress of the trip should quickly disappear.

He needs lots of human contact, affection, handling and exposure to other animals.

Once your pup has received his necessary vaccinations, feel free to take him out and about (on his lead, of course). Walk him around the neighbourhood, take him on your daily errands, let people pet him, let him meet other dogs and pets, etc. Puppies do not have to try to make friends; there will be no shortage of people who will want to introduce themselves. Just make sure that you carefully supervise each meeting. If the neighbour-hood children want to say hello, for example, that is great—children and pups most often make great companions. Sometimes an excited child can unintentionally handle a pup too roughly, or an overzealous pup can playfully nip a little too hard. You want to make socialisation experiences positive ones. What a pup learns during this very formative stage will affect his attitude toward future encounters. You want your dog to be comfort-able around everyone. A pup that has a bad experience with a child may grow up to be a dog that is shy around or aggressive toward children.

CONSISTENCY IN TRAINING

Dogs, being pack animals, naturally need a leader, or else they try to establish dominance in

Training Tip

Training your puppy takes much patience and can be frustrating at times, but you should see results from your efforts. If you have a puppy that seems untrainable, take him to a trainer or behaviourist. The dog may have a personality problem that requires the help of a professional, or perhaps you need help in learning how to train your dog.

their packs. When you bring a dog into your family, the choice of who becomes the leader and who becomes the 'pack' is entirely up to you! Your pup's intuitive quest for dominance, coupled with the fact that it is nearly impossible to look at an adorable Neapolitan Mastiff pup, with his 'puppy-dog' eyes and his too-big-for his-head-still-floppy ears, and not cave in, give the pup almost an unfair advantage in getting the upper hand! A pup will definitely test the waters to see what he can and cannot do. Do not give in to those pleading eyes—stand your ground when it comes to disciplining the pup and make sure that all family members do the same. It will only confuse the pup when Mother tells him to get off the sofa when he is used to sitting up there with Father to watch the nightly news. Avoid discrepancies by having all members of the household decide

becomes the adult dog's bad habit. There are some problems that are especially prevalent in puppies as they develop.

NIPPING

As puppies start to teethe, they feel the need to sink their teeth into anything available...unfortunately that includes your fingers, arms, hair, and toes. You may find this behaviour cute for the first five seconds...until you feel just how sharp those puppy teeth are. This is something you want to discourage immediately and consistently with a firm 'No!' (or whatever number of

It's up to you to decide if you want to allow your dog on the furniture. Once your Neo reaches full size, he may not leave any room on the sofa for you!

on the rules before the pup even comes home...and be consistent in enforcing them! Early training shapes the dog's personality, so you cannot be unclear in what you expect.

COMMON PUPPY PROBLEMS
The best way to prevent puppy problems is to be proactive in stopping an undesirable behaviour as soon as it starts. The old saying 'You can't teach an old dog new tricks' does not necessarily hold true, but it is true that it is much easier to discourage bad behaviour in a young developing pup than to wait until the pup's bad behaviour

Did You Know?

The majority of problems that are commonly seen in young pups will disappear as your dog gets older. However, how you deal with problems when he is young will determine how he reacts to discipline as an adult dog. It is important to establish who is boss (hopefully it will be you!) right away when you are first bonding with your dog. This bond will set the tone for the rest of your life together.

Chewing Tips

Chewing goes hand in hand with nipping in the sense that a teething puppy is always looking for a way to soothe his aching gums. In this case, instead of chewing on you, he may have taken a liking to your favourite shoe or something else which he should not be chewing. Again, realise that this is a normal canine behaviour that does not need to be discouraged, only redirected. Your pup just needs to be taught what is acceptable to chew on and what is off limits. Consistently tell him NO when you catch him chewing on something forbidden and give him a chew toy. Conversely, praise him when you catch him chewing on something appropriate. In this way you are discouraging the inappropriate behaviour and reinforcing the desired behaviour. The puppy chewing should stop after his adult teeth have come in, but an adult dog continues to chew for various reasons—perhaps because he is bored, perhaps to relieve tension or perhaps he just likes to chew. That is why it is important to redirect his chewing when he is still young.

is young, it can become dangerous as your Neapolitan Mastiff's adult teeth grow in and his jaws develop if he continues to think it is okay to gnaw on human appendages. Your Neapolitan Mastiff does not mean any harm with a friendly nip, but he also does not know his own strength.

Part of the socialisation process is allowing your Neo puppy to meet other dogs and pets. This should always be done under your supervision.

firm 'No's it takes for him to understand that you mean business). Then replace your finger with an appropriate chew toy. Whilst this behaviour is merely annoying when the dog

Neapolitan Mastiff

The first few days in your home are somewhat scary for a young pup; they are an adjustment period for him. Make the transition as smooth as possible with gentle handling, attention and affection.

CRYING/WHINING

Your pup will often cry, whine, whimper, howl or make some type of commotion when he is left alone. This is basically his way of calling out for attention to make sure that you know he is there and that you have not forgotten about him. He feels insecure when he is left alone, when you are out of the house and he is in his crate or when you are in another part of the house and he cannot see you. The noise he is making is an expression of the anxiety he feels at being alone, so he needs to be taught that being alone is okay. You are not actually training the dog to stop making noise, you are training him to feel comfortable when he is alone and thus removing the need for him to make the noise. This is where the crate filled with cosy bedding and a toy comes in handy. You want to know that he is safe when you are not there to supervise, and you

know that he will be safe in his crate rather than roaming freely about the house. In order for the pup to stay in his crate without making a fuss, he needs to be comfortable in his crate. On that note, it is extremely important that the crate is never used as a form of punishment, or the pup will have a negative association with the crate.

Accustom the pup to the crate in short, gradually increasing time intervals in which you put him in the crate, maybe with a treat, and stay in the room with him. If he cries or makes a fuss, do not go to him, but stay in his sight.

Gradually he will realise that staying in his crate is all right without your help, and it will not be so traumatic for him when you are not there. You may want to leave the radio on softly when you leave the house; the sound of human voices may be comforting to him.

Your Neo cannot be properly trained without using a suitable crate. Once he is used to it, the crate can be used to keep your Neo safe indoors or outdoors.

DIETARY AND FEEDING CONSIDERATIONS

Neapolitan adults should be fed two times a day and puppies three times a day until they are six months old. Free feeding of the Neapolitan is never recommended. The Neapolitan, from my experience, will consume anywhere from two to six pounds of dry kibble each day, some individuals eating more or less than others. I am an advocate of feeding either cooked beef, lamb or pork livers, kidneys and hearts and sometimes chicken made into a stew and spooned over the dog's kibble. This constitutes only ten percent of the entire meal. I also incorporate vegetables into their diets. Recently, I began adding a porridge made of oats, bran, brown rice and either cracked wheat, barley or blue corn

> **Did You Know?**
>
> You must store your dried dog food carefully. Open packages of dog food quickly lose their vitamin value, usually within 90 days of being opened. Mould spores and vermin could also contaminate the food.

meal to their kibble, while still feeding the meat stew and vegetables. If this method is followed, the amount of kibble can be decreased to offset the incorporation of the porridge.

A kibble that is higher in fat and carbohydrates but lower in protein is recommended for the Neapolitan after eight weeks of age. A high-protein diet has been found to contribute to skeletal problems. Too much weight too quickly on a fast growing puppy like the Neapolitan can cause severe bone and joint deformities and cause him to go down on his pasterns. All puppies are genetically programmed to be a certain size. This size should be reached by providing the puppy with proper nutrition, but it should be noted that a puppy lacking the genes for heavy bone and stockiness can be force-fed and still

> **Did You Know?**
>
> A good test for proper diet is the colour, odour and firmness of your dog's stool. A healthy dog usually produces three semi-hard stools per day. The stools should have no unpleasant odour. They should be the same colour from excretion to excretion.

never achieve the massiveness desired in the Neapolitan.

Today the choices of food for your Neapolitan Mastiff are many and varied. There are simply dozens of brands of food in all sorts of flavours and textures, ranging from puppy diets to those for seniors. There are even hypoallergenic and low-calorie diets available. Because your

Food Preference

Selecting the best dried dog food is difficult. There is no majority consensus amongst veterinary scientists as to the value of nutrient analyses (protein, fat, fibre, moisture, ash, cholesterol, minerals, etc.). All agree that feeding trials are what matters, but you also have to consider the individual dog. Its weight, age, activity and what pleases its taste, all must be considered. It is probably best to take the advice of your veterinary surgeon. Every dog's dietary requirements vary, even during the lifetime of a particular dog.

If your dog is fed a good dried food, it does not require supplements of meat or vegetables. Dogs do appreciate a little variety in their diets so you may choose to stay with the same brand, but vary the flavour. Alternatively you may wish to add a little flavoured stock to give a difference to the taste.

Neapolitan Mastiff's food has a bearing on coat, health and temperament, it is essential that the most suitable diet is selected for a Neapolitan Mastiff of his age. It is fair to say, however, that even dedicated owners can be somewhat perplexed by the enormous range of foods available. Only understanding what is best for your dog will help you reach a valued decision.

Dog foods are produced in three basic types: dried, semi-moist and tinned. Dried foods are useful for the cost-conscious for overall they tend to be less expensive than semi-moist or tinned. These contain the least fat

A puppy diet is different than an adult diet. Discuss the proper diet for your Neo with your vet or the breeder from whom you purchased the puppy.

63

Did You Know?

Some experts in canine health advise that stress during a dog's early years of development can compromise and weaken his immune system and may trigger the potential for a shortened life expectancy. They emphasise the need for happy and stress-free growing-up years.

Your pup should have a designated area in which he eats his meals; this should be in a place like the kitchen, not your sofa. Do not get in the habit of 'catering' to your pup; this puts him in control.

and the most preservatives. In general tinned foods are made up of 60–70 percent water, whilst semi-moist ones often contain so much sugar that they are perhaps the least preferred by owners,

even though their dogs seem to like them.

When selecting your dog's diet, three stages of development must be considered: the puppy stage, adult stage and the senior or veteran stage.

PUPPY STAGE

Puppies instinctively want to suck milk from their mother's teats and a normal puppy will exhibit this behaviour from just a few moments following birth. If puppies do not attempt to suckle within the first half-hour or so, they should be encouraged to do so by placing them on a nipple, having selected ones with plenty

of milk. This early milk supply is important in providing colostrum to protect the puppies during the first eight to ten weeks of their lives. Although a mother's milk is much better than any milk formula, despite there being some excellent ones available, if the puppies do not feed you will have to feed them yourself. For those with less experience, advice from a veterinary surgeon is important so that you feed not only the right quantity of milk but that of correct quality, fed at suitably frequent intervals, usually every two hours during the first few days of life.

Puppies should be allowed to nurse from their mothers for about

Grain-Based Diets

Many adult diets are based on grain. There is nothing wrong with this as long as it does not contain soy meal. Diets based on soy often cause flatulence (passing gas).

Grain-based diets are almost always the least expensive and a good grain diet is just as good as the most expensive diet containing animal protein.

There are many cases, however, when your dog might require a special diet. These special requirements should only be recommended by your veterinary surgeon.

A litter of Neo pups, still with the breeder. The breeder will keep the pups with their mother until they are weaned. Only after they are fully weaned and eating solid food are they considered old enough to go to new homes.

Did You Know?

Dog food must be at room temperature, neither too hot nor too cold. Fresh water, changed daily and served in a clean bowl, is mandatory, especially when feeding dried food.

Never feed your dog from the table while you are eating. Never feed your dog leftovers from your own meal. They usually contain too much fat and too much seasoning.

Dogs must chew their food. Hard pellets are excellent; soups and slurries are to be avoided.

Don't add leftovers or any extras to normal dog food. The normal food is usually balanced and adding something extra destroys the balance.

Except for age-related changes, dogs do not require dietary variations. They can be fed the same diet, day after day, without their becoming ill.

Whether puppy or adult, your Neo's diet will vary depending on how much activity he gets. A more active dog will require more calories, and vice versa.

the first six weeks, although from the third or fourth week you will have begun to introduce small portions of suitable solid food. Most breeders like to introduce alternate milk and meat meals initially, building up to weaning time.

By the time the puppies are seven or a maximum of eight weeks old, they should be fully weaned and fed solely on a proprietary puppy food. Selection of the most suitable, good-quality diet at this time is essential for a puppy's fastest growth rate is during the first year of life. Veterinary surgeons are usually able to offer advice in this regard and, the frequency of meals will have been reduced over time. When a young Neapolitan has reached the age of about three months an adult diet can be fed. Neapolitans grow rapidly but don't overfeed your puppy as gaining too much weight too fast can lead to bone and joint problems. Puppy and junior diets should be well balanced for the needs of your dog, so that except in certain

What are you feeding your dog?

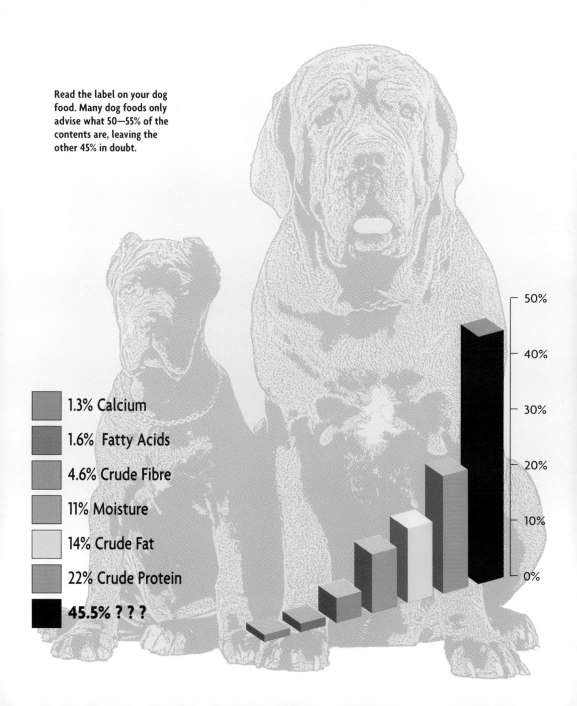

Read the label on your dog food. Many dog foods only advise what 50—55% of the contents are, leaving the other 45% in doubt.

1.3% Calcium

1.6% Fatty Acids

4.6% Crude Fibre

11% Moisture

14% Crude Fat

22% Crude Protein

45.5% ? ? ?

50%

40%

30%

20%

10%

0%

circumstances additional
vitamins, minerals and proteins
will not be required. Protein
content should not exceed 24%.

ADULT DIETS

A dog is considered an adult
when it has stopped growing, but
in general the diet of a
Neapolitan Mastiff can be
changed to an adult one at about
three months of age. Again you
should rely upon your veterinary
surgeon or dietary specialist to
recommend an acceptable
maintenance diet. Major dog food
manufacturers specialise in this
type of food, and it is just
necessary for you to select the
one best suited to your dog's
needs. Active dogs may have
different requirements than
sedate dogs. Neapolitan Mastiffs
do well when a small amount
(10%) of organ meat is added to
their diet. A Neapolitan Mastiff
reaches adulthood at about two
years of age, though some dogs
fully mature at 16 months and
others may take up to three years.

SENIOR DIETS

As dogs get older, their metabo-
lism changes. The older dog
usually exercises less, moves
more slowly and sleeps more.
This change in lifestyle and
physiological performance
requires a change in diet. Since
these changes take place slowly,
they might not be recognisable.

Do Dogs Have Taste Buds?

Watching a dog 'wolf' or gobble his
food, seemingly without chewing,
leads an owner to wonder whether
their dogs can taste anything. Yes,
dogs have taste buds, with sensory
perception of sweet, salty and sour.
Puppies are born with fully mature
taste buds.

What is easily recognisable is
weight gain. By continuing to
feed your dog an adult-mainte-
nance diet when it is slowing
down metabolically, your dog
will gain weight. Obesity in an
older dog compounds the health
problems that already accompany
old age.

As your dog gets older, few of
their organs function up to par.
The kidneys slow down and the
intestines become less efficient.
These age-related factors are best
handled with a change in diet
and a change in feeding schedule
to give smaller portions that are
more easily digested.

There is no single best diet
for every older dog. Whilst many
dogs do well on light or senior
diets, other dogs do better on
puppy diets or other special
premium diets such as lamb and
rice. Be sensitive to your senior
Neapolitan Mastiff's diet and this
will help control other problems
that may arise with your old
friend.

WATER

The Neapolitan requires large amounts of water and clean, fresh water should always be available. During housebreaking it is necessary to keep an eye on how much water your Neapolitan Mastiff is drinking, but once he is reliably trained he should have access to clean fresh water at all times. Water is just as essential a 'nutrient' as anything the dog obtains in his diet. Water keeps the dog's body properly hydrated and promotes normal function of the body's systems.

Water should be changed frequently, at least twice a day, as the Neapolitan deposits a slime in it after drinking, which I compare to the consistency of egg whites. Neapolitans love to drink and with saliva and water dripping from their pendulous lips, they cannot resist the urge to come and

put their head on your lap. Towels specifically relegated to the duty of mopping up water and food from the Neapolitan's lips, flews and dewlap seem to do the trick.

EXERCISE

All dogs require some form of exercise, regardless of breed. A sedentary lifestyle is as harmful to a dog as it is to a person. The Neapolitan Mastiff is an inactive breed that does not require much exercise, so you definitely do not have to be an Olympic athlete to provide your dog with the exercise he needs. Regular walks, play sessions in the garden or letting the dog run free in the garden under your supervision are sufficient forms of exercise for the Neapolitan Mastiff. For those who are more ambitious, you will find that your Neapolitan Mastiff also enjoys long walks. Bear in mind

Your Neo should always have access to water, especially when outside on a hot day. Water should be changed frequently and the water bowl kept clean.

Electrical Fencing

The electrical fencing system which forms an invisible fence works on a battery-operated collar that shocks the dog if it gets too close to the buried (or elevated) wire. There are some people who think very highly of this system of controlling a dog's wandering. Keep in mind that the collar has batteries. For safety's sake, replace the batteries every month with the best quality batteries available.

69

GROOMING

BRUSHING

A natural bristle brush or a hound glove can be used for regular routine brushing. Brushing is effective for removing dead hair and stimulating the dog's natural oils to add shine and a healthy look to the coat. The Neapolitan Mastiff's coat is short and dense, and should be brushed weekly as part of routine maintenance. Weekly brushing will get rid of dust and dandruff and remove any dead hair. Regular grooming sessions are also a good way to spend time with your dog. Many dogs grow to like the feel of being brushed and will enjoy the daily routine.

Grooming Equipment

How much grooming equipment you purchase will depend on how much grooming you are going to do. Here are some basics:
- Natural bristle brush
- Slicker brush
- Metal comb
- Scissors
- Blaster
- Rubber mat
- Dog shampoo
- Spray hose attachment
- Ear cleaner
- Cotton wipes
- Towels
- Nail clippers

Teaching your Neo to heel on lead is a necessity or you will find it very difficult to take him for walks. Exercise is important for your dog, just as it is for you.

that an overweight dog should never be suddenly over-exercised; instead he should be allowed to increase exercise slowly. Not only is exercise essential to keep the dog's body fit, it is essential to his mental well being. A bored dog will find something to do, which often manifests itself in some type of destructive behaviour. In this sense, it is essential for the owner's mental well being as well!

BATHING

Dogs do not need to be bathed as often as humans, but regular bathing is essential for healthy skin and a healthy, shiny coat. The Neapolitan's abundant loose skin requires cleaning and frequent baths. Again, like most anything, if you accustom your pup to being bathed as a puppy, it will be second nature by the time he grows up. You want your dog to be at ease in the bath or else it could end up a wet, soapy, messy ordeal for both of you!

Brush your Neapolitan Mastiff thoroughly before wetting his coat. Make sure that your dog has a good non-slip surface to stand on. Begin by wetting the dog's

Grooming Tips

Once you are sure that the dog is thoroughly rinsed, squeeze the excess water out of the coat with your hand and dry him with a heavy towel. You may choose to use a blaster on his coat or just let it dry naturally. In cold weather, never allow your dog outside with a wet coat.

There are 'dry bath' products on the market, which are sprays and powders intended for spot cleaning, that can be used between regular baths, if necessary. They are not substitutes for regular baths, but they are easy to use for touch-ups as they do not require rinsing.

Your Neo's coat should be brushed on a weekly basis to remove dead hair and to stimulate the skin. Accustom your Neo to routine grooming while he is still a pup.

coat. A shower or hose attachment is necessary for thoroughly wetting and rinsing the coat. Check the water temperature to make sure that it is neither too hot nor too cold.

Next, apply shampoo to the dog's coat and work it into a good lather. You should purchase a shampoo that is made for dogs. Do not use a product made for human hair. Wash the head last; you do not want shampoo to drip into the dog's eyes whilst you are washing the rest of his body. Work the shampoo all the way down to the skin. You can use this opportunity to check the skin for any bumps, bites or other abnormalities. Do not neglect any area of the body—get all of the hard-to-reach places.

Once the dog has been thoroughly shampooed, he requires an equally thorough rinsing. Shampoo left in the coat can be irritating to the skin. Protect his eyes from the shampoo

by shielding them with your hand and directing the flow of water in the opposite direction. You should also avoid getting water in the ear canal. Be prepared for your dog to shake out his coat—you might want to stand back, but make sure you have a hold on the dog to keep him from running through the house.

EAR CLEANING

The ears should be kept clean and any excess hair inside the ear should be carefully cut. Ears can be cleaned with a cotton wool bud and special cleaner or ear powder made especially for dogs. Be on the lookout for any signs of infection or ear mite infestation. If your Neapolitan Mastiff has been shaking his head or scratching at his ears frequently, this usually indicates a problem. If his ears have an unusual odour, this is a sure sign of mite infestation or infection, and a signal to have his ears checked by the veterinary surgeon.

NAIL CLIPPING

Your Neapolitan Mastiff should be accustomed to having his nails trimmed at an early age, since it will be part of your maintenance routine throughout his life. Not only does it look nicer, but long nails can be sharp if they scratch someone unintentionally. Also, a long nail has a better chance of ripping and bleeding, or causing

Did You Know?

The use of human soap products like shampoo, bubble bath and hand soap can be damaging to a dog's coat and skin. Human products are too strong and remove the protective oils coating the dog's hair and skin (making him water-resistant). Use only shampoo made especially for dogs and you may like to use a medicated shampoo, which will always help to keep external parasites at bay.

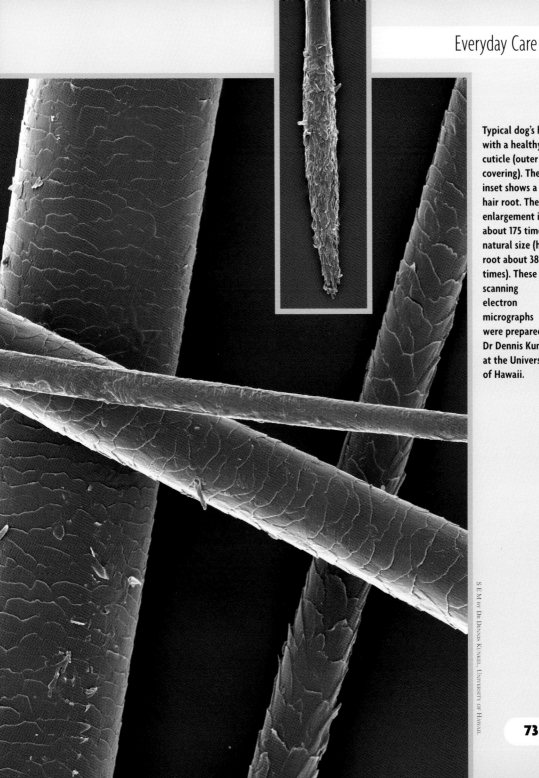

Typical dog's hair with a healthy cuticle (outer covering). The inset shows a hair root. The enlargement is about 175 times natural size (hair root about 38 times). These scanning electron micrographs were prepared by Dr Dennis Kunkel at the University of Hawaii.

S E M by Dr Dennis Kunkel, University of Hawaii.

Your Neo's ears can be cleaned with special wipes available from your local pet shop. Inspect your Neo's ears for ear mites or signs of infection.

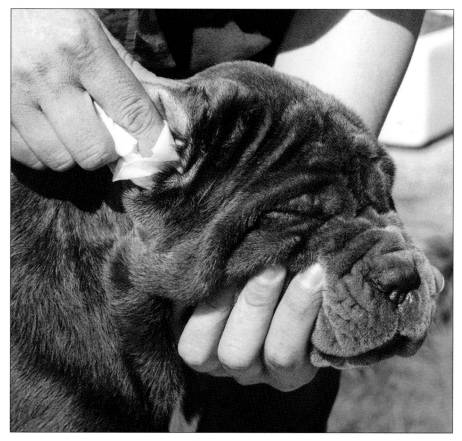

the feet to spread. A good rule of thumb is that if you can hear your dog's nails clicking on the floor when he walks, his nails are too long.

Before you start cutting, make sure you can identify the 'quick' in each nail. The quick is a blood vessel that runs through the centre of each nail and grows rather close to the end. It will bleed if accidentally cut, which will be quite painful for the dog as it contains nerve endings. Keep some type of clotting agent on hand, such as a styptic pencil or styptic powder (the type used for shaving). This will stop the bleeding quickly when applied to the end of the cut nail. Do not panic if this happens, just stop the bleeding and talk soothingly to your dog. Once he has calmed down, move on to the next nail. It is better to clip a little at a time, particu-

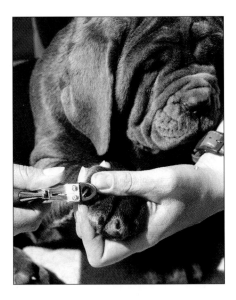

larly with black-nailed dogs.

Hold your pup steady as you begin trimming his nails; you do not want him to make any sudden movements or run away. Talk to him soothingly and stroke him as you clip. Holding his foot in your hand, simply take off the end of each nail in one quick clip. You can purchase nail clippers that are specially made for dogs; you can probably find them wherever you buy pet or grooming supplies.

TRAVELLING WITH YOUR DOG

CAR TRAVEL
You should accustom your Neapolitan Mastiff to riding in a car at an early age. You may or may not take him in the car often, but at the very least he will need to go to the vet and you do not

Nail Maintenance

Nail Casing

Quick

Cut Line

Dark-Coloured Nails

With black or dark nails, where the quick is difficult to see, it's best to clip only the tip of the nail or to use a file.

Light-Coloured Nails

In light-coloured nails, clipping is much simpler because you can see the vein (or quick) that grows inside the casing.

Special nail clippers for dogs are available from your local pet shop.

Clip only the bottom portion of the nail, avoiding the quick. If you cut into the quick, the nail will bleed and the dog will experience pain. A styptic pencil will stop the bleeding. Reassure the injured dog by talking quietly to him.

75

Neapolitan Mastiff

The Neo's loose skin requires special attention. Cleaning between the wrinkles on the face is demonstrated here.

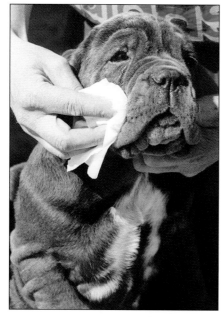

very dangerous! If you should stop short, your dog can be thrown and injured. If the dog starts climbing on you and pestering you whilst you are driving, you will not be able to concentrate on the road. It is an unsafe situation for everyone—human and canine.

For long trips, be prepared to stop to let the dog relieve himself. Bring along whatever you need to clean up after him. You should take along some paper kitchen towels and perhaps some old towelling for use should he have an accident in the car or suffer from travel

You should transport your Neo puppy in a crate in the rear of your vehicle. Never allow any dog to be loose whilst you are driving.

want these trips to be traumatic for the dog or a big hassle for you. The safest way for a dog to ride in the car is in his crate. If he uses a crate in the house, you can use the same crate for travel, if your vehicle can accommodate it. You may need a van or station wagon for transporting an adult Neapolitan. Put the pup in the crate and see how he reacts. If the puppy seems uneasy, you can have a passenger hold him on his lap whilst you drive but you will need to find another solution before your dog is fully grown. Another option is a specially made safety harness for dogs, which straps the dog in much like a seat belt. Do not let the dog roam loose in the vehicle—this is

Travel Tip

Never leave your dog alone in the car. In hot weather your dog can die from the high temperature inside a closed vehicle; even a car parked in the shade can heat up very quickly. Leaving the window open is dangerous as well since the dog can hurt himself trying to get out.

Travel Tip

If you are going on a long motor trip with your dog, be sure the hotels are dog friendly. Many hotels do not accept dogs. Also take along some ice that can be thawed and offered to your dog if he becomes overheated. Most dogs like to lick ice.

sickness. If you are travelling in warm weather, always have water to offer your pet.

AIR TRAVEL

Whilst it is possible to take a dog on a flight within Britain, this is fairly unusual and advance permission is always required. The dog will be required to travel in a fibreglass crate and you should always check in advance with the airline regarding specific requirements. To help the dog be at ease, put one of his favourite toys in the crate with him. Do not feed the dog for at least six hours

Travel Tip

When travelling, never let your dog off-lead in a strange area. Your dog could run away out of fear or decide to chase a passing squirrel or cat or simply want to stretch his legs without restriction—you might never see your canine friend again.

before the trip to minimise his need to relieve himself. However, certain regulations specify that water must always be made available to the dog in the crate.

Make sure your dog is properly identified and that your contact information appears on his ID tags and on his crate. Animals travel in a different area of the plane than human passen-

Whenever you must crate your dog, he should always be allowed out on a regular basis so he can relieve himself.

gers so every rule must be strictly adhered to so as to prevent the risk of getting separated from your dog.

BOARDING

So you want to take a family holiday—and you want to include all members of the family. You would probably make arrangements for

Travel Tip

For international travel you will have to make arrangements well in advance (perhaps months), as countries' regulations pertaining to bringing in animals differ. There may be special health certificates and/or vaccinations that your dog will need before taking the trip; sometimes this has to be done within a certain time frame. In rabies-free countries, you will need to bring proof of the dog's rabies vaccination and there may be a quarantine period upon arrival.

accommodations ahead of time anyway, but this is especially important when travelling with a dog. You do not want to make an overnight stop at the only place around for miles and find out that they do not allow dogs. Also, you do not want to reserve a place for your family without confirming that you are travelling with a dog because if it is against their policy you may not have a place to stay.

Alternatively, if you are travelling and choose not to bring your Neapolitan Mastiff, you will have to make arrangements for him whilst you are away. Some options are to take him to a neighbour's house to stay whilst you are gone, to have a trusted neighbour stop by often or stay at your house,

or bring your dog to a reputable boarding kennel. If you choose to board him at a kennel, you should visit in advance to see the facility, how clean they are and where the dogs are kept. Talk to some of the employees and see how they treat the dogs—do they spend time with the dogs, play with them, exercise them, etc.? Also find out the kennel's policy on vaccinations and what they require. This is for all of the dogs' safety, since when dogs are kept together, there is a greater risk of diseases being passed from dog to dog.

IDENTIFICATION

Your Neapolitan Mastiff is your valued companion and friend. That is why you always keep a close eye on him and you have made sure that he cannot escape from the garden or wriggle out of his collar and run away from you. However, accidents can happen and there may come a time when your dog unexpectedly gets separated from you. If this unfortunate event should occur, the first thing on your mind will be finding him. Proper identification, including an ID tag, a tattoo, and possibly a microchip, will increase the chances of his being returned to you safely and quickly.

Did You Know?

As puppies become more and more expensive, especially those puppies of high quality for showing and/or breeding, they have a greater chance of being stolen. The usual collar dog tag is, of course, easily removed. But there are two techniques that have become widely used for identification.

The puppy microchip implantation involves the injection of a small microchip, about the size of a corn kernel, under the skin of the dog. If your dog shows up at a clinic or shelter, or is offered for resale under less than savoury circumstances, it can be positively identified by the microchip. The microchip is scanned and a registry quickly identifies you as the owner. This is not only protection against theft, but should the dog run away or go chasing a squirrel and get lost, you have a fair chance of getting it back.

Tattooing is done on various parts of the dog, from its belly to its cheeks. The number tattooed can be your telephone number or any other number which you can easily memorise. When professional dog thieves see a tattooed dog, they usually lose interest in it. Both microchipping and tattooing can be done at your local veterinary clinic. For the safety of our dogs, no laboratory facility or dog broker will accept a tattooed dog as stock.

If you are searching for a boarding kennel, look for one that is clean, with sufficient space to enable the Neo to walk around and get some exercise.

Living with an untrained dog is a lot like owning a piano that you do not know how to play—it is a nice object to look at but it does not do much more than that to bring you pleasure. Now try taking piano lessons and suddenly the piano comes alive and brings forth magical sounds and rhythms that set your heart singing and your body swaying.

The same is true with your Neapolitan Mastiff. Any dog is a big responsibility and if not trained sensibly may develop unacceptable behaviour that annoys you or could even cause family friction.

To train your Neapolitan

Mastiff, you may like to enrol in an obedience class. Teach him good manners as you learn how and why he behaves the way he does. Find out how to communicate with your dog and how to recognise and understand his communications with you. Suddenly the dog takes on a new role in your life—he is smart, interesting, well behaved and fun to be with. He demonstrates his bond of devotion to you daily. In other words, your Neapolitan Mastiff does wonders for your ego because he constantly reminds you that you are not only his leader, you are his hero!

Those involved with teaching dog obedience and counselling owners about their dogs' behaviour have discovered some interesting facts about dog ownership. For example, training dogs when they are puppies results in the highest rate of success in developing well-mannered and well-adjusted adult dogs. Training an older dog, from six months to six years of age, can produce almost equal results providing that the owner accepts the dog's slower rate of learning

Did You Know?

If you start with a normal, healthy dog and give him time, patience and some carefully executed lessons, you will reap the rewards of that training for the life of the dog. And what a life it will be! The two of you will find immeasurable pleasure in the companionship you have built together with love, respect and understanding.

Did You Know?

To a dog's way of thinking, your hands are like his mouth in terms of a defence mechanism. If you squeeze him too tightly, he might just bite you because that would be his normal response. This is not aggressive biting and, although all biting should be discouraged, you need the discipline in learning how to handle your dog.

capability and is willing to work patiently to help the dog succeed at developing to his fullest potential. Unfortunately, many owners of untrained adult dogs lack the patience factor, so they do not persist until their dogs are successful at learning particular behaviours.

Training a puppy, aged 10 to 16 weeks (20 weeks at the most) is like working with a dry sponge in a pool of water. The pup soaks up whatever you show him and constantly looks for more things to do and learn. At this early age, his body is not yet producing hormones, and therein lies the reason for such a high rate of success. Without hormones, he is focused on his owners and not particularly interested in investigating other places, dogs, people, etc. You are his leader: his provider of food, water, shelter and security. He latches onto you and wants to stay close. He will

usually follow you from room to room, will not let you out of his sight when you are outdoors with him, and will respond in like manner to the people and animals you encounter. If you greet a friend warmly, he will be happy to greet the person as well. If, however, you are hesitant, even anxious, about the approach of a stranger, he will respond accordingly.

Once the puppy begins to produce hormones, his natural

If you have a securely fenced garden, you may choose to feed your Neo outdoors. An advantage is that the dog will have immediate access to his relief area when he is finished eating.

Training Tip

Training a dog is a life experience. Many parents admit that much of what they know about raising children they learned from caring for their dogs. Dogs respond to love, fairness and guidance, just as children do. Become a good dog owner and you may become an even better parent.

curiosity emerges and he begins to investigate the world around him. It is at this time when you may notice that the untrained dog begins to wander away from you and even ignore your commands to stay close.

There are usually classes within a reasonable distance of the owner's home, but you also must put in the time between sessions to practise with your Neapolitan at home. Sometimes there are classes available but the tuition is too costly. Whatever the circumstances, the solution to your training problems lies within the pages of this book.

This chapter is devoted to helping you train your Neapolitan Mastiff at home. If the recommended procedures are followed faithfully, you may expect positive results that will prove rewarding to both you and your dog.

Whether your new charge is a puppy or a mature adult, the

Mealtime

Mealtime should be a peaceful time for your puppy. Do not put his food and water bowls in a high-traffic area in the house. For example, give him his own little corner of the kitchen where he can eat undisturbed and where he will not be under foot. Do not allow small children or other family members to disturb the pup when he is eating.

methods of teaching and the techniques we use in training basic behaviours are the same. After all, no dog, whether puppy or adult, likes harsh or inhumane methods. All creatures, however, respond favourably to gentle motivational methods and sincere praise and encouragement. Now let us get started.

HOUSEBREAKING

You can train a puppy to relieve itself wherever you choose, but this must be somewhere suitable. You should bear in mind from the outset that when your puppy is old enough to go out in public places, any canine deposits must be removed at once. You will always have to carry with you a small plastic bag or 'poop-scoop.'

Outdoor training includes such surfaces as grass, dirt and cement. Indoor training usually means training your

Think Before You Bark!

Dogs are sensitive to their master's moods and emotions. Use your voice wisely when communicating with your dog. Never raise your voice at your dog unless you are angry and trying to correct him. 'Barking' at your dog can become as meaningless as 'dogspeak' is to you. Think before you bark!

Did You Know?

Dogs will do anything for your attention. If you reward the dog when he is calm and resting, you will develop a well-mannered dog. If, on the other hand, you greet your dog excitedly and encourage him to wrestle and roughhouse with you, the dog will greet you the same way and you will have a hyper dog on your hands.

dog to newspaper.

When deciding on the surface and location that you will want your Neapolitan Mastiff to use, be sure it is going to be permanent. Training your dog to grass and then changing your mind two months later is extremely difficult for both dog and owner.

Next, choose the command you will use each and every time you want your puppy to void. 'Go hurry up' and 'Toilet' are examples of commands commonly used by dog owners.

Get in the habit of giving the puppy your chosen relief command before you take him out. That way, when he becomes an adult, you will be able to determine if he wants to go out when you ask him. A confirmation will be signs of interest, wagging his tail, watching you intently, going to the door, etc.

PUPPY'S NEEDS
Puppy needs to relieve himself after play periods, after each meal, after he has been sleeping and any time he indicates that he is

You can train your Neo to relieve himself in whatever area and on whatever type of surface you choose. Make your choice carefully, as once he is trained you will have a hard time convincing him to go elsewhere.

Did You Know?

Dogs are the most honourable animals in existence. They consider another species (humans) as their own. They interface with you. You are their leader. Puppies perceive children to be on their level; their actions around small children are different from their behaviour around their adult masters.

Clean up after your Neo. Your local pet shop should have a poop scoop device to assist you in this task.

Do not get in the habit of carrying your pup to his relief area. Take him there on lead and keep visits to the relief site as short as possible.

looking for a place to urinate or defecate.

The urinary and intestinal tract muscles of very young puppies are not fully developed. Therefore, like human babies, puppies need to relieve themselves frequently.

Take your puppy out often—every hour for an eight-week-old, for example, and always immediately after sleeping and eating. The older the puppy, the less often he will need to relieve himself. Finally, as a mature healthy adult, he will require only three to five relief trips per day.

HOUSING

Since the types of housing and control you provide for your puppy has a direct relationship on the success of housetraining, we consider the various aspects of both before we begin training.

Bringing a new puppy home and turning him loose in your house can be compared to turning a child loose in a sports arena and telling the child that the place is all his! The sheer enormity of the place would be too much for him to handle.

Instead, offer the puppy clearly defined areas where he can play, sleep, eat and live. A room of the house where the family gathers is the most obvious

CANINE DEVELOPMENT SCHEDULE

It is important to understand how and at what age a puppy develops into adulthood. If you are a puppy owner, consult the following Canine Development Schedule to determine the stage of development your puppy is currently experiencing. This knowledge will help you as you work with the puppy in the weeks and months ahead.

Period	Age	Characteristics
FIRST TO THIRD	BIRTH TO SEVEN WEEKS	Puppy needs food, sleep and warmth, and responds to simple and gentle touching. Needs mother for security and disciplining. Needs littermates for learning and interacting with other dogs. Pup learns to function within a pack and learns pack order of dominance. Begin socialising with adults and children for short periods. Begins to become aware of its environment.
FOURTH	EIGHT TO TWELVE WEEKS	Brain is fully developed. Needs socialising with outside world. Remove from mother and littermates. Needs to change from canine pack to human pack. Human dominance necessary. Fear period occurs between 8 and 16 weeks. Avoid fright and pain.
FIFTH	THIRTEEN TO SIXTEEN WEEKS	Training and formal obedience should begin. Less association with other dogs, more with people, places, situations. Period will pass easily if you remember this is pup's change-to-adolescence time. Be firm and fair. Flight instinct prominent. Permissiveness and over-disciplining can do permanent damage. Praise for good behaviour.
JUVENILE	FOUR TO EIGHT MONTHS	Another fear period about 7 to 8 months of age. It passes quickly, but be cautious of fright and pain. Sexual maturity reached. Dominant traits established. Dog should understand sit, down, come and stay by now.

NOTE: THESE ARE APPROXIMATE TIME FRAMES. ALLOW FOR INDIVIDUAL DIFFERENCES IN PUPPIES.

choice. Puppies are social animals and need to feel a part of the pack right from the start. Hearing your voice, watching you whilst you are doing things and smelling you nearby are all positive reinforcers that he is now a member of your pack. Usually a family room, the kitchen or a nearby adjoining breakfast area is ideal for providing safety and security for

both puppy and owner.

Within that room there should be a smaller area which the puppy can call his own. An alcove, a wire or fibreglass dog crate or a fenced (not boarded!) corner from

The Golden Rule

The golden rule of dog training is simple. For each 'question' (command), there is only one correct answer (reaction). One command = one reaction. Keep practising the command until the dog reacts correctly without hesitating. Be repetitive but not monotonous. Dogs get bored just as people do!

Training Tip

Stand up straight and authoritatively when giving your dog commands. Do not issue commands when lying on the floor or lying on your back on the sofa. If you are on your hands and knees when you give a command, your dog will think you are positioning yourself to play.

which he can view the activities of his new family will be fine. The size of the area or crate is the key factor here. The area must be large enough for the puppy to lie down and stretch out as well as stand up without rubbing his head on the top, yet small enough so that he cannot relieve himself at one end and sleep at the other without coming into contact with his droppings until fully trained to relieve himself outside.

Dogs are, by nature, clean animals and will not remain close to their relief areas unless forced to do so. In those cases, they then become dirty dogs and usually remain that way for life.

The designated area should be lined with clean bedding and a toy. Water must always be available, in a non-spill container.

CONTROL
By control, we mean helping the puppy to create a lifestyle pattern

Housebreaking Tip

Do not carry your dog to his toilet area. Lead him there on a leash or, better yet, encourage him to follow you to the spot. If you start carrying him to his spot, you might end up doing this routine forever and your dog will have the satisfaction of having trained YOU.

that will be compatible to that of his human pack (YOU!). Just as we guide little children to learn our way of life, we must show the puppy when it is time to play, eat, sleep, exercise and even entertain himself.

Your puppy should always sleep in his crate. He should also learn that, during times of household confusion and excessive human activity such as at breakfast when family members are preparing for the day, he can play by himself in relative safety and comfort in his designated area. Each time you leave the puppy alone, he should understand exactly where he is to stay. You can gradually increase the time he is left alone to get him used to it. Puppies are chewers. They cannot tell the difference between lamp cords, television wires, shoes, table legs, etc. Chewing into a television wire, for example, can be fatal to the puppy whilst a shorted wire can start a fire in the house.

If the puppy chews on the arm of the chair when he is alone, you will probably discipline him

Practice Makes Perfect

• Have training lessons with your dog every day in several short segments—three to five times a day for a few minutes at a time is ideal.
• Do not have long practice sessions. The dog will become easily bored.
• Never practise when you are tired, ill, worried or in an otherwise negative mood. This will transmit to the dog and may have an adverse effect on its performance.

Think fun, short and above all POSITIVE! End each session on a high note, rather than a failed exercise, and make sure to give a lot of praise. Enjoy the training and help your dog enjoy it, too.

Whether housebreaking or teaching basic commands, puppies are most trainable at an early age. The training they receive and the things they experience when very young will leave a lasting impact throughout their lives.

An important step in housebreaking is teaching the difference between playtime and toilet time. The pup will learn to relieve himself quickly so that playtime can begin.

How Many Times a Day?

AGE	RELIEF TRIPS
To 14 weeks	10
14–22 weeks	8
22–32 weeks	6
Adulthood	4
(dog stops growing)	

These are estimates, of course, but they are a guide to the MINIMUM opportunities a dog should have each day to relieve itself.

angrily when you get home. Thus, he makes the association that your coming home means he is going to be punished. (He will not remember chewing up the chair and is incapable of making the association of the discipline with his naughty deed.)

Other times of excitement, such as family parties, etc., can be fun for the puppy providing he can view the activities from the security of his designated area. He is not underfoot and he is not being fed all sorts of titbits that

will probably cause him stomach distress, yet he still feels a part of the fun.

SCHEDULE
A puppy should be taken to his relief area each time he is released from his designated area, after meals, after a play session, when he first awakens in the morning (at age eight weeks, this can mean 5 a.m.!). The puppy will indicate that he's ready 'to go' by circling or sniffing busily—-do not misinterpret these signs. For a puppy less than ten weeks of age, a routine of taking him out every hour is necessary. As the puppy grows, he will be able to wait for longer periods of time.

Keep trips to his relief area short. Stay no more than five or six minutes and then return to the house. If he goes during that time, praise him lavishly and take him indoors immediately. If he does not, but he has an accident when you go back indoors, pick him up immediately, say 'No! No!' and return to his relief area. Wait a few minutes, then return to the house again. Never hit a puppy or rub his face in urine or excrement when he has an accident!

Once indoors, put the puppy in his crate until you have had time to clean up his accident. Then release him to the family area and watch him more

closely than before. Chances are, his accident was a result of your not picking up his signal or waiting too long before offering him the opportunity to relieve himself. Never hold a grudge against the puppy for accidents.

Let the puppy learn that going outdoors means it is time to relieve himself, not play. Once trained, he will be able to play indoors and out and still differentiate between the times for play versus the times for relief.

Help him develop regular hours for naps, being alone, playing by himself and just resting, all in his crate. Encourage him to entertain himself whilst you are busy with your activities. Let him learn that having you near is comforting, but it is not your main purpose in life to provide him with undivided attention.

Each time you put a puppy in his own area, use the same command, whatever suits best. Soon, he will run to his crate or special area when he hears you say those words.

Crate training provides safety for you, the puppy and the home. It also provides the puppy with a feeling of security, and that helps the puppy achieve self-confidence and

The Success Method

Success that comes by luck is usually short lived. Success that comes by well-thought-out proven methods is often more easily achieved and permanent. This is the Success Method. It is designed to give you, the puppy owner, a simple yet proven way to help your puppy develop clean living habits and a feeling of security in his new environment.

THE SUCCESS METHOD

1 Tell the puppy 'Crate time!' and place him in the crate with a small treat (a piece of cheese or half of a biscuit). Let him stay in the crate for five minutes while you are in the same room. Then release him and praise lavishly. Never release him when he is fussing. Wait until he is quiet before you let him out.

2 Repeat Step 1 several times a day.

3 The next day, place the puppy in the crate as before. Let him stay there for ten minutes. Do this several times.

4 Continue building time in five-minute increments until the puppy

stays in his crate for 30 minutes with you in the room. Always take him to his relief area after prolonged periods in his crate.

5 Now go back to Step 1 and let the puppy stay in his crate for five minutes, this time while you are out of the room.

6 Once again, build crate time in five-minute increments with you out of the room. When the puppy will stay willingly in his crate (he may even fall asleep!) for 30 minutes with you out of the room, he will be ready to stay in it for several hours at a time.

6 Steps to Successful Crate Training

Did You Know?

The puppy should also have regular play and exercise sessions when he is with you or a family member. Exercise for a very young puppy can consist of a short walk around the house or garden. Playing can include fetching games with a large ball or a special raggy. (All puppies teethe and need soft things upon which to chew.) Remember to restrict play periods to indoors within his living area (the family room, for example) until he is completely housetrained.

It is an absolute necessity with such a large breed for the Neo owner to be in complete control when the dog is on lead.

clean habits.

Remember that one of the primary ingredients in housetraining your puppy is control. Regardless of your lifestyle, there will always be occasions when you will need to have a place where your dog can stay and be happy and safe. Training is the answer for now and in the future.

In conclusion, a few key elements are really all you need for a successful housetraining method—consistency, frequency, praise, control and supervision. By following these procedures with a normal, healthy puppy, you and the puppy will soon be past the stage of 'accidents' and ready to move on to a full and rewarding life together.

Housebreaking Tip

Most of all, be consistent. Always take your dog to the same location, always use the same command, and always have him on lead when he is in his relief area, unless a fenced-in garden is available.

By following the Success Method, your puppy will be completely housetrained by the time his muscle and brain development reach maturity. Keep in mind that small breeds usually mature faster than large breeds, but all puppies should be trained by six months of age.

Use only the strongest collars and leads for your Neo. These Neos are already massive, and they are not yet full grown! Venere della Grotta Azzurra (left) is seven months old, and Vera della Grotta Azzurra is six months old. Owned by La Tutela Kennels.

ROLES OF DISCIPLINE, REWARD AND PUNISHMENT

Discipline, training one to act in accordance with rules, brings order to life. It is as simple as

Did You Know?

Never train your dog, puppy or adult, when you are angry or in a sour mood. Dogs are very sensitive to human feelings, especially anger, and if your dog senses that you are angry or upset, he will connect your anger with his training and learn to resent or fear his training sessions.

that. Without discipline, particularly in a group society, chaos reigns supreme and the group will eventually perish. Humans and canines are social animals and need some form of discipline in order to function effectively. They must procure food, protect their home base and their young and reproduce to keep the species going.

If there were no discipline in the lives of social animals, they would eventually die from starvation and/or predation by other stronger animals.

In the case of domestic canines, dogs need discipline in their lives in order to understand

how their pack (you and other family members) functions and how they must act in order to survive.

A large humane society in a highly populated area recently surveyed dog owners regarding their satisfaction with their relationships with their dogs. People who had trained their dogs were 75% more satisfied with their pets than those who had never trained their dogs.

Dr. Edward Thorndike, a psychologist, established *Thorndike's Theory of Learning*, which states that a behaviour that results in a pleasant event tends to be repeated. A behaviour that results in an unpleasant event tends not to be repeated. It is this theory on which training methods are based today. For example, if you manipulate a dog to perform a specific behaviour and reward him for doing it, he is likely to do it again because he enjoyed the end result.

Occasionally, punishment, a penalty inflicted for an offence, is necessary. The best type of punishment often comes from an outside source. For example, a child is told not to touch the stove because he may get burned. He disobeys and touches the stove. In doing so, he receives a burn. From that time on, he respects the heat of the stove and avoids contact with it. Therefore, a behaviour that results in an unpleasant event

tends not to be repeated.

A good example of a dog learning the hard way is the dog who chases the house cat. He is told many times to leave the cat alone, yet he persists in teasing the cat. Then, one day he begins chasing the cat but the cat turns and swipes a claw across the dog's face, leaving him with a painful gash on his nose. The final result is that the dog stops chasing the cat.

TRAINING EQUIPMENT

COLLAR AND LEAD
For a Neapolitan Mastiff the collar and lead that you use for training must be one with which you are easily able to work, not too heavy for the dog and perfectly safe. If your dog pulls mightily on the leash, you may require a chain choker collar.

TREATS
Have a bag of treats on hand. Something nutritious and easy to swallow works best. Use a soft treat, a chunk of cheese or a piece

> **Did You Know?**
>
> Dogs are as different from each other as people are. What works for one dog may not work for another. Have an open mind. If one method of training is unsuccessful, try another.

93

If your Neo responds to food like these two 'chow-hounds,' you will probably have an easy time training your dog by using treats as rewards.

of cooked chicken rather than a dry biscuit. By the time the dog gets done chewing a dry treat, he will forget why he is being rewarded in the first place! Using food rewards will not teach a dog to beg at the table—the only way to teach a dog to beg at the table is to give him food from the table. In training, rewarding the dog with a food treat will help him associate praise and the treats with learning new behaviours that obviously please his owner.

TRAINING BEGINS: ASK THE DOG A QUESTION

In order to teach your dog anything, you must first get his attention. After all, he cannot learn anything if he is looking away from you with his mind on something else.

To get his attention, ask him, 'School?' and immediately walk over to him and give him a treat as you tell him 'Good dog.' Wait a minute or two and repeat the routine, this time with a treat in your hand as you approach within a foot of the dog. Do not go directly to him, but stop about a foot short of him and hold out the treat as you ask, 'School?' He will see you approaching with a treat in your hand and most likely begin walking toward you. As you meet, give him the treat and praise again.

The third time, ask the question, have a treat in your hand and walk only a short distance toward the dog so that he must walk almost all the way to you. As he reaches you, give him the treat and praise again.

By this time, the dog will probably be getting the idea that if he pays attention to you, especially when you ask that question, it will pay off in treats and fun activities for him. In other words, he learns that 'school' means doing fun things with you that result in treats and positive attention for him.

Remember that the dog does not understand your verbal language, he only recognises sounds. Your question translates to a series of sounds for him, and those sounds become the signal to go to you and pay attention; if he does, he will get to interact with you plus receive treats and praise.

THE BASIC COMMANDS

TEACHING SIT

Now that you have the dog's attention, attach his lead and hold it in your left hand and a food treat in your right. Place your food hand at the dog's nose and let him lick the treat but not take it from you. Say 'Sit' and slowly raise your food hand from in front of the dog's nose up over his head so that he is looking at the ceiling. As he bends his head upward, he will have to bend his knees to maintain his balance. As he bends his knees, he will assume a sit position. At that point, release the

When introducing the sit command, you may have to physically guide your dog into the correct position for the first few tries.

food treat and praise lavishly with comments such as 'Good dog! Good sit!', etc. Remember to always praise enthusiastically, because dogs relish verbal praise from their owners and feel so proud of themselves whenever they accomplish a behaviour.

You will not use food forever in getting the dog to obey your commands. Food is only used to teach new behaviours, and once the dog knows what you want when you give a specific command, you will wean him off of the food treats but still maintain the verbal praise. After all, you will always have your voice with you, and there will be

Every Neo must be taught to sit upon command. This is one of the most basic commands.

A young Neo demonstrates how well he has learned his first lesson...sit.

you say 'Down' or he attempts to snap at the person who tries to force him down.

Have the dog sit close alongside your left leg, facing in the same direction as you are. Hold the lead in your left hand and a food treat in your right. Now place your left hand lightly on the top of the dog's shoulders where they meet above the spinal cord. Do not push down on the dog's shoulders; simply rest your left hand there so you can guide the dog to lie down close to your left leg rather than to swing away from your side when he drops.

Now place the food hand at the dog's nose, say 'Down' very softly (almost a whisper), and slowly lower the food hand to the dog's front feet. When the food

many times when you have no food rewards but expect the dog to obey.

TEACHING DOWN

Teaching the down exercise is easy when you understand how the dog perceives the down position, and it is very difficult when you do not. Dogs perceive the down position as a submissive one, therefore teaching the down exercise using a forceful method can sometimes make the dog develop such a fear of the down that he either runs away when

Did You Know?

Dogs do not understand our language. They can be trained to react to a certain sound, at a certain volume. If you say 'No, Oliver' in a very soft pleasant voice it will not have the same meaning as 'No, Oliver!!' when you shout it as loud as you can. You should never use the dog's name during a reprimand, just the command NO!! Since dogs don't understand words, comics often use dogs trained with opposite meanings. Thus, when the comic commands his dog to SIT the dog will stand up, and vice versa.

hand reaches the floor, begin moving it forward along the floor in front of the dog. Keep talking softly to the dog, saying things like, 'Do you want this treat? You can do this, good dog.' Your reassuring tone of voice will help calm the dog as he tries to follow the food hand in order to get the treat.

When the dog's elbows touch the floor, release the food and praise softly. Try to get the dog to maintain that down position for several seconds before you let him sit up again. The goal here is to get the dog to settle down and not feel threatened in the down position.

TEACHING STAY

It is easy to teach the dog to stay in either a sit or a down position. Again, we use food and praise during the teaching process as we help the dog to understand

Did You Know?

If you want to be successful in training your dog, you have four rules to obey yourself:
1. Develop an understanding of how a dog thinks.
2. Do not blame the dog for lack of communication.
3. Define your dog's personality and act accordingly.
4. Have patience and be consistent.

Did You Know?

A dog in jeopardy never lies down. He stays alert on his feet because instinct tells him that he may have to run away or fight for his survival. Therefore, if a dog feels threatened or anxious, he will not lie down. Consequently, it is important to have the dog calm and relaxed as he learns the down exercise.

exactly what it is that we are expecting him to do.

To teach the sit/stay, start with the dog sitting on your left side as

Teaching down may be difficult at first. Your Neo may need some extra coaxing to assume the position, which is viewed by dogs as a submissive posture.

Teach your Neo to stay. It is not a difficult exercise, and it can be taught with a combination of voice commands and hand signals.

before and hold the lead in your left hand. Have a food treat in your right hand and place your food hand at the dog's nose. Say 'Stay' and step out on your right foot to stand directly in front of the dog, toe to toe, as he licks and nibbles the treat. Be sure to keep his head facing upward to maintain the sit position. Count to five and then swing around to stand next to the dog again with him on your left. As soon as you get back to the original position, release the food and praise lavishly.

To teach the down/stay, do the down as previously described. As soon as the dog lies down, say 'Stay' and step

Training Tip

Play fetch games with your puppy in an enclosed area where he can retrieve his toy and bring it back to

you. Always use a toy or object designated just for this purpose. Never use a shoe, stocking or other item he may later confuse with those in your wardrobe or underneath your chair.

out on your right foot just as you did in the sit/stay. Count to five and then return to stand beside the dog with him on your left side. Release the treat and praise as always.

Within a week or ten days, you can begin to add a bit of distance between you and your dog when you leave him. When you do, use your left hand open with the palm facing the dog as a stay signal, much the same as the hand signal a police officer uses to stop traffic at an intersection. Hold the food treat in your right hand as before, but this time the food is not touching the dog's nose. He will watch the food hand and quickly learn that he is going to get that treat as soon as you return to his side.

When you can stand 1 metre away from your dog for 30 seconds, you can then begin building time and distance in both stays. Eventually, the dog can be expected to remain in the stay position for prolonged periods of time until you return to him or call him to you. Always praise lavishly when he stays.

TEACHING COME

If you make teaching 'come' a fun experience, you should never have a 'student' that does not love the game or that fails to come when called. The secret, it seems, is never to teach the word 'come.'

At times when an owner most wants his dog to come when called, the owner is likely

Training Tip

Never call your dog to come to you for a correction or scold him when he reaches you. That is the quickest way to turn a 'Come' command into 'Go away fast!' Dogs think only in the present tense, and your dog will connect the scolding with coming to you, not with the misbehaviour of a few moments earlier.

upset or anxious and he allows these feelings to come through in the tone of his voice when he calls his dog. Hearing that desperation in his owner's voice, the dog fears the results of going to him and therefore either disobeys outright or runs in the opposite direction. The secret, therefore, is to teach the dog a game and, when you want him to come to you, simply play the game. It is practically a no-fail solution!

To begin, have several members of your family take a few food treats and each go into a different room in the house. Take turns calling the dog, and each person should celebrate the dog's finding him with a treat and lots of happy praise. When a person calls the dog, he is actually inviting the dog to find him and get a treat as a reward for 'winning.'

A few turns of the 'Where are you?' game and the dog will figure out that everyone is playing the game and that each person has a big celebration awaiting his success at locating them. Once he learns to love the game, simply calling out 'Where are you?' will bring him running from wherever he is when he hears that all-important question.

The come command is recognised as one of the most important things to teach a dog,

You certainly should teach your Neo to come when called. Greet your pup with praise and petting, and he should always want to run to you.

but there are trainers who work with thousands of dogs and never teach the actual word 'Come.' Yet these dogs will race to respond to a person who uses the dog's name followed by 'Where are you?' For example, a woman has a 12-year-old companion dog who went blind, but who never fails to locate her owner when asked, 'Where are you?'

Children particularly love to play this game with their dogs. Children can hide in smaller places like a shower or bathtub, behind a bed or under a table. The dog needs to work a little bit harder to find these hiding places, but when he does he loves to celebrate with a treat and a tussle with a favourite youngster.

TEACHING HEEL

Heeling means that the dog walks beside the owner without pulling. It takes time and patience on the owner's part to succeed at teaching the dog that he (the owner) will not proceed unless the dog is walking calmly beside him. Pulling out

ahead on the lead is definitely not acceptable.

Begin with holding the lead in your left hand as the dog sits beside your left leg. Move the loop end of the lead to your right hand but keep your left hand short on the lead so it keeps the dog in close next to you.

Say 'Heel' and step forward on your left foot. Keep the dog close to you and take three steps. Stop and have the dog sit next to you in what we now call the 'heel position.' Praise verbally, but do not touch the dog. Hesitate a moment and begin again with 'Heel,' taking three steps and stopping, at which point the dog is told to sit again.

Your goal here is to have the dog walk those three steps without pulling on the lead. When he will walk calmly beside you for three steps

Training Tip

When calling the dog, do not say 'Come.' Say things like, 'Rover, where are you? See if you can find me! I have a biscuit for you!' Keep up a constant line of chatter with coaxing sounds and frequent questions such as, 'Where are you?' The dog will learn to follow the sound of your voice to locate you and receive his reward.

Training Tip

Teach your dog to HEEL in an enclosed area. Once you think the dog will obey reliably and you want to attempt advanced obedience exercises such as off-lead heeling, test him in a fenced-in area so he cannot run away.

With a dog as large as a Neo, he must be taught to walk alongside you without pulling or stopping. The heel exercise is required; the dog must learn to walk at your pace and stop when you stop.

without pulling, increase the number of steps you take to five. When he will walk politely beside you whilst you take five steps, you can increase the length of your walk to ten steps. Keep increasing the length of your stroll until the dog will walk quietly beside you without pulling as long as you want him to heel. When you stop heeling, indicate to the dog that the exercise is over by verbally praising as you pet him and say 'OK, good dog.' The 'OK' is used as a release word meaning that the exercise is finished and the dog is free to relax.

If you are dealing with a dog who insists on pulling you around, simply 'put on your brakes' and stand your ground until the dog realises that the two of you are not going anywhere until he is beside you and moving at your pace, not his. It may take some time just standing there to convince the dog that you are the leader and you will be the one to decide on the direction and speed of your travel.

Each time the dog looks up at you or slows down to give a slack lead between the two of you, quietly praise him and say, 'Good heel. Good dog.' Eventually, the dog will begin to respond and within a few days he will be walking politely beside you without pulling on the lead. At first, the training sessions should be kept short

101

and very positive; soon the dog will be able to walk nicely with you for increasingly longer distances. Remember also to give the dog free time and the opportunity to run and play when you are done with heel practice.

WEANING OFF FOOD IN TRAINING

Food is used in training new behaviours. Once the dog understands what behaviour goes with a specific command, it is time to start weaning him off the food treats. At first, give a treat after each exercise. Then, start to give a treat only after every other exercise. Mix up the times when you offer a food reward and the times when you only offer praise so that the dog will never know when he is going to receive both food and praise and when he is going to receive only praise. This is

> **Training Tip**
>
> If you begin teaching the heel by taking long walks and letting the dog pull you along, he misinterprets this action as an acceptable form of taking a walk. When you pull back on the lead to counteract his pulling, he reads that tug as a signal to pull even harder!

> **Training Tip**
>
> If you are walking your dog and he suddenly stops and looks straight into your eyes, ignore him. Pull the leash and lead him into the direction you want to walk.

called a variable ratio reward system and it proves successful because there is always the chance that the owner will produce a treat, so the dog never stops trying for that reward. No matter what, ALWAYS give verbal praise.

OBEDIENCE CLASSES

It is a good idea to enrol in an obedience class if one is available in your area. If yours is a show dog, ringcraft classes would be more appropriate. Many areas have dog clubs that offer basic obedience training as well as preparatory classes for obedience competition. There are also local dog trainers who offer similar classes.

At obedience trials, dogs can earn titles at various levels of competition. The beginning levels of competition include basic behaviours such as sit, down, heel, etc. The more advanced levels of competition include jumping, retrieving, scent discrimination and signal work. The advanced levels require a dog and owner to put a lot of time and effort into their training and the titles that can be earned at these levels of competition are very prestigious.

OTHER ACTIVITIES FOR LIFE

Whether a dog is trained in the structured environment of a class or alone with his owner at home, there are many activities that can bring fun and rewards to both owner and dog once they have mastered basic control.

Teaching the dog to help out around the home, in the garden or on the farm provides great satisfaction to both dog and owner. In addition, the dog's help makes life a little easier for his owner and raises his stature

Obedience School

A basic obedience beginner's class usually lasts for six to eight weeks. Dog and owner attend an hour-long lesson once a week and practise for a few minutes, several times a day, each day at home. If done properly, the whole procedure will result in a well-mannered dog and an owner who delights in living with a pet that is eager to please and enjoys doing things with his owner.

as a valued companion to his family. It helps give the dog a purpose by occupying his mind and providing an outlet for his energy.

Backpacking is an exciting and healthy activity that the dog can be taught without assistance from more than his owner. The exercise of walking and climbing is good for man and dog alike, and the bond that they develop together is priceless.

Did You Know?

Occasionally, a dog and owner who have not attended formal classes have been able to earn entry-level titles by obtaining competition rules and regulations from a local kennel club and practising on their own to a degree of perfection. Obtaining the higher level titles, however, almost always requires extensive training under the tutelage of experienced instructors. In addition, the more difficult levels require more specialised equipment whereas the lower levels do not.

Dog ownership opens up a world of new experiences for dog and owner. Contact a local kennel club to learn about the different activities in which you and your Neo can become involved.

103

Dogs suffer many of the same physical illnesses as people. They might even share many of the same psychological

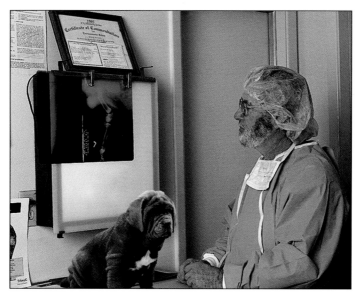

Take your Neo puppy to the local vet soon after you buy him to have his overall health assessed.

problems. Since people usually know more about human diseases than canine maladies, many of the terms used in this chapter will be familiar but not necessarily those used by veterinary surgeons. We will use the term *x-ray*, instead of the more acceptable term *radiograph*. We will also use the familiar term *symptoms* even though dogs don't have symptoms, which are verbal descriptions of the patient's feelings: dogs have *clinical signs*. Since dogs can't speak, we have to look for clinical signs...but we still use the term symptoms in this book.

As a general rule, medicine is practised. That term is not arbitrary. Medicine is a constantly changing art as we learn more and more about genetics, electronic aids (like CAT scans) and daily laboratory advances. There are many dog maladies, like canine hip dysplasia, which are not universally treated in the same manner. Some veterinary surgeons opt for surgery more often than others do.

SELECTING A VETERINARY SURGEON

Your selection of a veterinary surgeon should not be based upon personality (as most are) but upon their convenience to your home. You want a vet who is close because you might have emergencies or need to make multiple visits for treatments. You want a vet who has services that you might require such as tattooing and grooming facilities, as well as sophisticated pet supplies and a good reputation for ability and responsiveness. There is nothing more frustrating than having to wait a day or more to get a response from your veterinary surgeon.

All veterinary surgeons are licensed and their diplomas and/or certificates should be displayed in their waiting rooms. There are, however, many veterinary specialities that usually require further studies and internships. There are specialists in heart problems (veterinary cardiologists), skin problems (veterinary dermatologists), teeth and gum problems (veterinary dentists), eye problems (veterinary ophthalmologists), x-rays (veterinary radiologists), and surgeons who have specialities

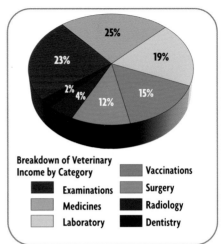

Breakdown of Veterinary Income by Category

- Examinations
- Medicines
- Laboratory
- Vaccinations
- Surgery
- Radiology
- Dentistry

A typical American vet's income categorised according to services performed. This survey dealt with small-animal (pet) practices.

in bones, muscles or other organs. Most veterinary surgeons do routine surgery such as neutering, stitching up wounds and docking tails for those breeds in which such is required for show purposes. When the problem affecting your dog is serious, it is not unusual or impudent to get another medical opinion, although in Britain you are obliged to advise the vets concerned about this. You might also want to compare costs amongst several veterinary surgeons. Sophisticated health care and veterinary services can be very costly. Don't be bashful about discussing these costs with your veterinary surgeon or his (her) staff. Important decisions are often based upon financial considerations.

Internal Organs with Skeletal Structure

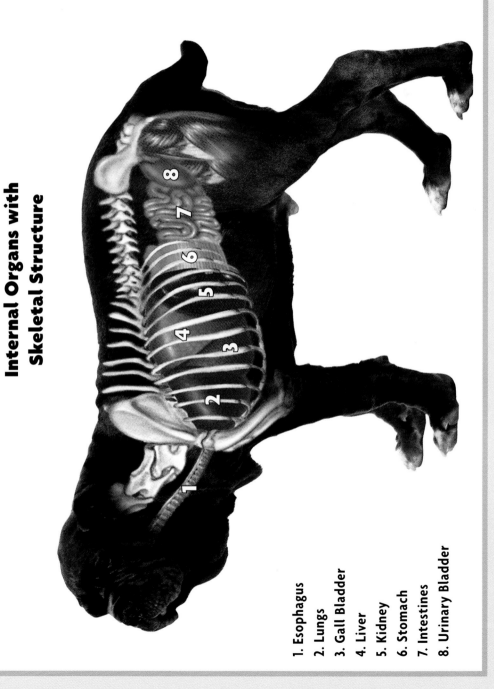

1. Esophagus
2. Lungs
3. Gall Bladder
4. Liver
5. Kidney
6. Stomach
7. Intestines
8. Urinary Bladder

PREVENTATIVE MEDICINE

It is much easier, less costly and more effective to practise preventative medicine than to fight bouts of illness and disease. Properly bred puppies come from parents that were selected based upon their genetic disease profile. Their mothers should have been vaccinated, free of all internal and external parasites, and properly nourished. For these reasons, a visit to the veterinary surgeon who cared for the dam (mother) is recommended. The dam can pass on disease resistance to her puppies, which can last for eight to ten weeks. She can also pass on parasites and many infections. That's why you should visit the veterinary surgeon who cared for the dam.

WEANING TO FIVE MONTHS OLD

Puppies should be weaned by the time they are about two months old. A puppy that remains for at least eight weeks

> **Did You Know?**
>
> Your veterinary surgeon will probably recommend that your puppy be vaccinated before you take him outside. There are airborne diseases, parasite eggs in the grass and unexpected visits from other dogs that might be dangerous to your puppy's health.

> **Did You Know?**
>
> It was announced in April 1999 that the severe quarantine laws imposed on animals entering Britain from other rabies-free countries would become a thing of the past by April 2001. Rather than being confined to a kennel for six months upon arrival in Britain, animals undergo a series of blood tests and vaccinations, and are identifed by microchip implantation. Qualified pets receive a 'health passport' that allows their owners to travel with them between Britain and other (mostly European) countries in which rabies does not exist.
>
> Animals from countries such as the United States and Canada, where rabies is a problem, still will be subject to quarantine. Although veterinary standards are high in these countries, recently infected dogs may test negative to the disease and, without the quarantine period, may unknowingly introduce rabies into previously unaffected countries.

with its mother and litter mates usually adapts better to other dogs and people later in its life.

Some new owners have their puppy examined by a veterinary surgeon immediately, which is a good idea. Vaccination programmes usually begin when the puppy is very young.

First Aid at a Glance

Burns
Place the affected area under cool water; use ice if only a small area is burnt.

Bee/Insect bites
Apply ice to relieve swelling; antihistamine dosed properly.

Animal bites
Clean any bleeding area; apply pressure until bleeding subsides; go to the vet.

Spider bites
Use cold compress and a pressurised pack to inhibit venom's spreading.

Antifreeze poisoning
Immediately induce vomiting by using hydrogen peroxide.

Fish hooks
Removal best handled by vet; hook must be cut in order to remove.

Snake bites
Pack ice around bite; contact vet quickly; identify snake for proper antivenin.

Car accident
Move dog from roadway with blanket; seek veterinary aid.

Shock
Calm the dog, keep him warm; seek immediate veterinary help.

Nosebleed
Apply cold compress to the nose; apply pressure to any visible abrasion.

Bleeding
Apply pressure above the area; treat wound by applying a cotton pack.

Heat stroke
Submerge dog in cold bath; cool down with fresh air and water; go to the vet.

Frostbite/Hypothermia
Warm the dog with a warm bath, electric blankets or hot water bottles.

Abrasions
Clean the wound and wash out thoroughly with fresh water; apply antiseptic.

 Remember: an injured dog may attempt to bite a helping hand from fear and confusion. Always muzzle the dog before trying to offer assistance.

The puppy will have its teeth examined and have its skeletal conformation and general health checked prior to certification by the veterinary surgeon. Puppies in certain breeds have problems with their kneecaps, eye cataracts and other eye problems, heart murmurs and undescended testicles. They may also have personality problems and your veterinary surgeon might have training in temperament evaluation.

VACCINATION SCHEDULING
Most vaccinations are given by injection and should only be done by a veterinary surgeon. Both you and he should keep a record of the date of the injection, the identification of the vaccine and the amount given. Some vets give a first vaccination at eight weeks, but most dog breeders prefer the course not to commence until about ten weeks because of negating any antibodies passed on by the dam. The vaccination scheduling is usually based on a 15-day cycle. You must take your vet's advice as to when to vaccinate as this may differ according to the vaccine used. Most vaccinations immunise your puppy against viruses.

The usual vaccines contain immunising doses of several different viruses such as distemper, parvovirus, parainfluenza and hepatitis. There are other vaccines available when the puppy is at risk. You should rely upon professional advice. This is especially true for the booster-shot programme. Most vaccination programmes require a booster when the puppy is a year old and once a year

Did You Know?

Vaccines do not work all the time. Sometimes dogs are allergic to them and many times the antibodies, which are supposed to be stimulated by the vaccine, just are not produced. You should keep your dog in the veterinary clinic for an hour after it is vaccinated to be sure there are no allergic reactions.

HEALTH AND VACCINATION SCHEDULE

AGE IN WEEKS:	6TH	8TH	10TH	12TH	14TH	16TH	20-24TH	1 YR
Worm Control	✔	✔	✔	✔	✔	✔	✔	
Neutering								✔
Heartworm*		✔		✔		✔	✔	
Parvovirus	✔		✔		✔		✔	✔
Distemper		✔		✔		✔		✔
Hepatitis		✔		✔		✔		✔
Leptospirosis								✔
Parainfluenza	✔		✔		✔			✔
Dental Examination		✔					✔	✔
Complete Physical		✔					✔	✔
Coronavirus				✔			✔	✔
Kennel Cough	✔							
Hip Dysplasia								✔
Rabies*							✔	

Vaccinations are not instantly effective. It takes about two weeks for the dog's immunisation system to develop antibodies. Most vaccinations require annual booster shots. Your veterinary surgeon should guide you in this regard.
*Not applicable in the United Kingdom

thereafter. In some cases, circumstances may require more frequent immunizations.

Kennel cough, more formally known as tracheobron-chitis, is treated with a vaccine that is sprayed into the dog's nostrils. Kennel cough is usually included in routine vaccination, but this is often not so effective as for other major diseases.

FIVE MONTHS TO ONE YEAR OF AGE
Unless you intend to breed or show your dog, neutering the puppy at six months of age is recommended. Discuss this with your veterinary surgeon; most professionals advise neutering the puppy. Neutering has proven to be extremely beneficial to both male and female puppies. Besides eliminating the possibility of pregnancy, it inhibits (but does not prevent) breast cancer in bitches and prostate cancer in male dogs. It

Did You Know?

Male dogs are neutered. The operation removes the testicles and requires that the dog be anaesthetised. Recovery takes about one week. Females are spayed. This is major surgery and it usually takes a bitch two weeks to recover.

is very rare to diagnose breast cancer in a female dog who was spayed at or before about nine months of age before her first heat.

Your veterinary surgeon should provide your puppy with a thorough dental evaluation at six months of age, ascertaining whether all the permanent teeth have erupted properly. A home dental care regimen should be initiated at six months, including brushing weekly and providing good dental devices (such as nylon bones). Regular dental care promotes healthy teeth, fresh breath and a longer life.

ONE TO SEVEN YEARS
Once a year, your grown dog should visit the vet for an examination and vaccination boosters. Some vets recommend blood tests, thyroid level check and dental evaluation to accompany these annual visits. A thorough clinical evaluation by the vet can provide critical background information for your

DISEASE REFERENCE CHART

	What is it?	What causes it?	Symptoms
Leptospirosis	Severe disease that affects the internal organs; can be spread to people.	A bacterium, which is often carried by rodents, that enters through mucous membranes and spreads quickly throughout the body.	Range from fever, vomiting and loss of appetite in less severe cases to shock, irreversible kidney damage and possibly death in most severe cases.
Rabies	Potentially deadly virus that infects warm-blooded mammals. Not seen in United Kingdom.	Bite from a carrier of the virus, mainly wild animals.	1st stage: dog exhibits change in behaviour, fear. 2nd stage: dog's behaviour becomes more aggressive. 3rd stage: loss of coordination, trouble with bodily functions.
Parvovirus	Highly contagious virus, potentially deadly.	Ingestion of the virus, which is usually spread through the faeces of infected dogs.	Most common: severe diarrhoea. Also vomiting, fatigue, lack of appetite.
Kennel cough	Contagious respiratory infection.	Combination of types of bacteria and virus. Most common: *Bordetella bronchiseptica* bacteria and parainfluenza virus.	Chronic cough.
Distemper	Disease primarily affecting respiratory and nervous system.	Virus that is related to the human measles virus.	Mild symptoms such as fever, lack of appetite and mucous secretion progress to evidence of brain damage, 'hard pad.'
Hepatitis	Virus primarily affecting the liver.	Canine adenovirus type I (CAV-1). Enters system when dog breathes in particles.	Lesser symptoms include listlessness, diarrhoea, vomiting. More severe symptoms include 'blue-eye' (clumps of virus in eye).
Coronavirus	Virus resulting in digestive problems.	Virus is spread through infected dog's faeces.	Stomach upset evidenced by lack of appetite, vomiting, diarrhoea.

dog. Blood tests are often performed at one year of age, and dental examinations around the third or fourth birthday. In the long run, quality preventive care for your pet can save money, teeth and lives.

SKIN PROBLEMS IN NEAPOLITAN MASTIFFS

Veterinary surgeons are consulted by dog owners for skin problems more than any other group of diseases or maladies. Dogs' skin is almost as sensitive as human skin and both suffer almost the same ailments (though the occurrence of acne in dogs is rare!). For this reason, veterinary dermatology has developed into a speciality practised by many veterinary surgeons.

Since many skin problems have visual symptoms that are almost identical, it requires the skill of an experienced veterinary dermatologist to identify and cure many of the more severe skin

disorders. Pet shops sell many treatments for skin problems but most of the treatments are directed at symptoms and not the underlying problem(s). If your dog is suffering from a skin disorder, you should seek professional assistance as quickly as possible. As with all diseases, the earlier a problem is identified and treated, the more successful is the cure.

INHERITED SKIN PROBLEMS

Many skin disorders are inherited and some are fatal. For example, acrodermatitis is an inherited disease that is transmitted by both parents. The parents, who appear (phenotypically) normal, have a recessive gene for acrodermatitis, meaning that they carry, but are not affected by the disease.

Acrodermatitis is just one example of how difficult it is to prevent congenital dog diseases. The cost and skills required to ascertain whether two dogs should be mated are too high even though puppies with acrodermatitis rarely reach two years of age.

Other inherited skin problems are usually not as fatal as acrodermatitis. All inherited diseases must be diagnosed and treated by a veterinary specialist. There are active programmes being undertaken by many veterinary

Did You Know?

Never allow your dog to swim in polluted water or public areas where water quality can be suspect. Even perfectly clear water can harbour parasites, many of which can cause serious to fatal illnesses in canines. Areas inhabited by waterfowl and other wildlife are especially dangerous.

pharmaceutical manufacturers to solve most, if not all, of the common skin problems of dogs.

PARASITE BITES

Many of us are allergic to insect bites. The bites itch, erupt and may even become infected. Dogs have the same reaction to fleas, ticks and/or mites. When an insect lands on you, you have the chance to whisk it away with your hand. Unfortunately, when our dog is bitten by a flea, tick or mite, it can only scratch it away or bite it. By the time the dog has been bitten, the parasite has done some of its damage. It may also have laid eggs to cause further problems in the near future. The itching from parasite bites is probably due to the saliva injected into the site when the parasite sucks the dog's blood.

AUTO-IMMUNE SKIN CONDITIONS

Auto-immune skin conditions are commonly referred to as being allergic to yourself, whilst allergies are usually inflammatory reactions to an outside

Did You Know?

There is a 25% chance of a puppy getting this fatal gene combination from two parents with recessive genes for acrodermatitis:

AA= NORMAL, HEALTHY
aa= FATAL
Aa= RECESSIVE, NORMAL
    APPEARING

If the female parent has an Aa gene and the male parent has an Aa gene, the chances are one in four that the puppy will have the fatal genetic combination aa.

	Dam		♀
	A	a	
A	AA	Aa	
a	Aa	aa	

(Sire / ♂)

Did You Know?

Chances are that you and your dog will have the same allergies. Your allergies are readily recognisable and usually easily treated. Your dog's allergies may be masked.

stimulus. Auto-immune diseases cause serious damage to the tissues that are involved.

The best known auto-immune disease is lupus, which affects people as well as dogs. The symptoms are variable and may affect the kidneys, bones, blood chemistry and skin. It can be fatal to both dogs and humans, though it is not thought to be transmissible. It is usually successfully treated with cortisone, prednisone or similar corticosteroid, but

Did You Know?

A dental examination is in order when the dog is between six months and one year of age so any permanent teeth that have erupted incorrectly can be corrected. It is important to begin a brushing

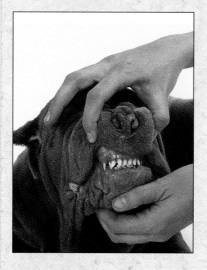

routine, preferably using a two-sided brushing technique, whereby both sides of the tooth are brushed at the same time. Durable nylon and safe edible chews should be a part of your puppy's arsenal for good health, good teeth and pleasant breath. The vast majority of dogs three to four years old and older has diseases of the gums from lack of dental attention. Using the various types of dental chews can be very effective in controlling dental plaque.

Acral lick is a poorly understood behaviour in which a dog, particularly of a large breed, constantly licks at a spot on his foreleg until the hair wears away and an open sore forms.

extensive use of these drugs can have harmful side effects.

ACRAL LICK DERMATITIS

Neapolitan Mastiffs and many other dogs have a very poorly understood syndrome called acral lick. The manifestation of the problem is the dog's tireless attack at a specific area of the body, almost always the legs. They lick so intensively that they remove the hair and skin leaving an ugly, large wound. There is no absolute cure, but corticosteroids are the most common treatment.

AIRBORNE ALLERGIES

An interesting allergy is pollen allergy. Humans have hay fever, rose fever and other fevers with which they suffer during the pollinating season. Many dogs suffer the same allergies. When the pollen count is high your dog might suffer, but don't expect him to sneeze and have a runny nose like a human would. Dogs react to pollen allergies the same way they

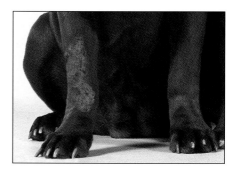

react to fleas—they scratch and bite themselves.

Dogs, like humans, can be tested for allergens. Discuss the testing with your veterinary dermatologist.

FOOD PROBLEMS

FOOD ALLERGIES
Dogs are allergic to many foods that are best-sellers and highly recommended by breeders and veterinary surgeons. Changing the brand of food that you buy may not eliminate the problem if the element to which the dog is allergic is contained in the new brand.

Recognising a food allergy is difficult. Humans vomit or have rashes when they eat a food to which they are allergic. Dogs neither vomit nor (usually) develop a rash. They react in the same manner as they do to an airborne or flea allergy: they itch, scratch and bite. Thus making the diagnosis extremely difficult. Whilst pollen allergies and parasite bites are usually seasonal, food allergies are year-round problems.

FOOD INTOLERANCE
Food intolerance is the inability of the dog to completely digest certain foods. Puppies that may have done very well on their mother's milk may not do well

on cow's milk. The result of this food intolerance may be loose bowels, passing gas and stomach pains. These are the only obvious symptoms of food intolerance and that makes diagnosis difficult.

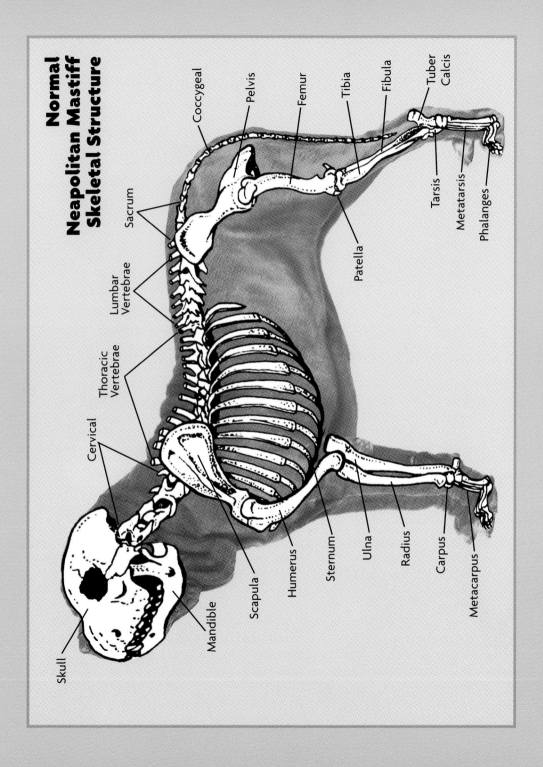

**Normal
Neapolitan Mastiff
Skeletal Structure**

Skull

Mandible

Scapula

Humerus

Sternum

Ulna

Radius

Carpus

Metacarpus

Cervical

Thoracic
Vertebrae

Lumbar
Vertebrae

Sacrum

Coccygeal

Pelvis

Femur

Tibia

Fibula

Patella

Tuber
Calcis

Tarsis

Metatarsis

Phalanges

Don't Eat the Daisies!

Many plants and flowers are beautiful to look at, but can be highly toxic if ingested by your dog. Reactions range from abdominal pain and vomiting to convulsions and death. If the following plants are in your home, remove them. If they are outside your house or in your garden, avoid accidents by making sure your dog is never left unsupervised in those locations.

Azalea	Dumb cane	Mescal bean
Belladonna	Dutchman's breeches	Mushrooms
Bird of Paradise	Elephant's ear	Nightshade
Bulbs	Hydrangea	Philodendron
Calla lily	Jack-in-the-pulpit	Poinsettia
Cardinal flower	Jasmine	Prunus species
Castor bean	Jimsonweed	Tobacco
Chinaberry tree	Larkspur	Yellow jasmine
Daphne	Laurel	Yews, Taxus species
	Lily of the valley	

TREATING FOOD PROBLEMS

It is possible to handle food allergies and food intolerance yourself. Put your dog on a diet that it has never had. Obviously if it has never eaten this new food it can't have been allergic or intolerant of it. Start with a single ingredient that is not in the dog's diet at the present time. Ingredients like chopped beef or fish are common in dogs' diets, so try something more exotic like rabbit, pheasant or even just vegetables. Keep the dog on this diet (with no additives) for a month. If the symptoms of food allergy or intolerance disappear, chances are your dog has a food allergy.

Don't think that the single ingredient cured the problem.

You still must find a suitable diet and ascertain which ingredient in the old diet was objectionable. This is most easily done by adding ingredients to the new diet one at a time. Let the dog stay on the modified diet for a month before you add another ingredient. Eventually, you will determine the ingredient that caused the adverse reaction.

An alternative method is to carefully study the ingredients in the diet to which your dog is allergic or intolerant. Identify the main ingredient in this diet and eliminate the main ingredient by buying a different food that does not have that ingredient. Keep experimenting until the symptoms disappear after one month on the new diet.

A scanning electron micrograph (S. E. M.) of a dog flea, *Ctenocephalides canis*.

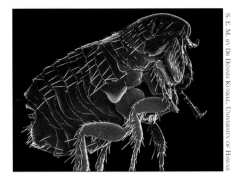

S. E. M. BY DR DENNIS KUNKEL, UNIVERSITY OF HAWAII

Opposite page: A scanning electron micrograph of a dog or cat flea, *Ctenocephalides*, magnified more than 100x. This has been colourized for effect.

EXTERNAL PARASITES

Of all the problems to which dogs are prone, none is more well known and frustrating than fleas. Flea infestation is relatively simple to cure but difficult to prevent. Parasites that are

harboured inside the body are a bit more difficult to eradicate but they are easier to control.

FLEAS

To control a flea infestation you have to understand the flea's life cycle. Fleas are often thought of as a summertime problem but centrally heated homes have changed the patterns and fleas can be found at any time of the year. The most effective method of flea control is a two-stage approach: one stage to kill the adult fleas, and the other to control the development of pre-adult fleas. Unfortunately, no single active ingredient is effective against all stages of the life cycle.

LIFE CYCLE STAGES

During its life, a flea will pass through four life stages: egg, larva, pupa and adult. The adult stage is the most visible and irritating stage of the flea life

Magnified head of a dog flea, *Ctenocephalides canis*.

Did You Know?

Fleas have been around for millions of years and have adapted to changing host animals.

They are able to go through a complete life cycle in less than one month or they can extend their lives to almost two years by remaining as pupae or cocoons. They do not need blood or any other food for up to 20 months.

They have been measured as being able to jump 300,000 times and can jump 150 times their length in any direction including straight up. Those are just a few of the reasons they are so successful in infesting a dog!

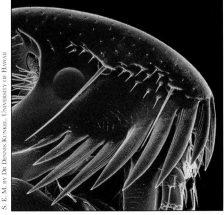

S. E. M. BY DR DENNIS KUNKEL, UNIVERSITY OF HAWAII

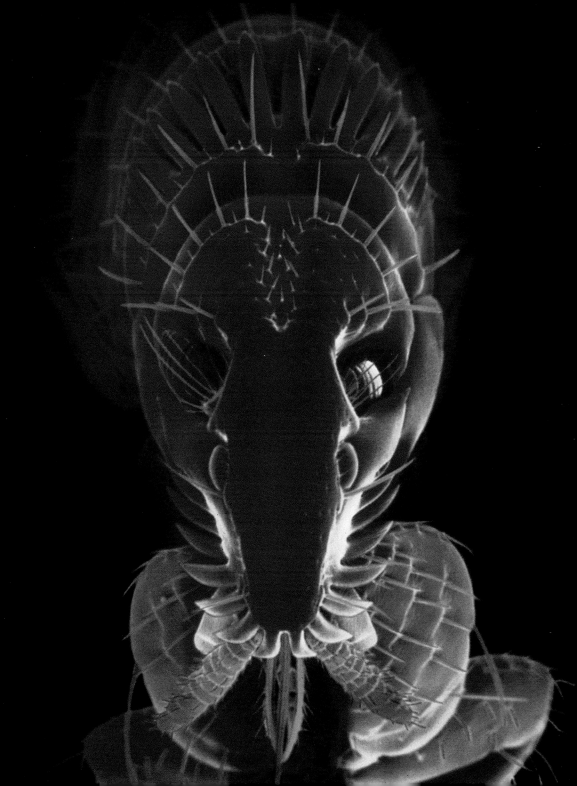

The Life Cycle of the Flea

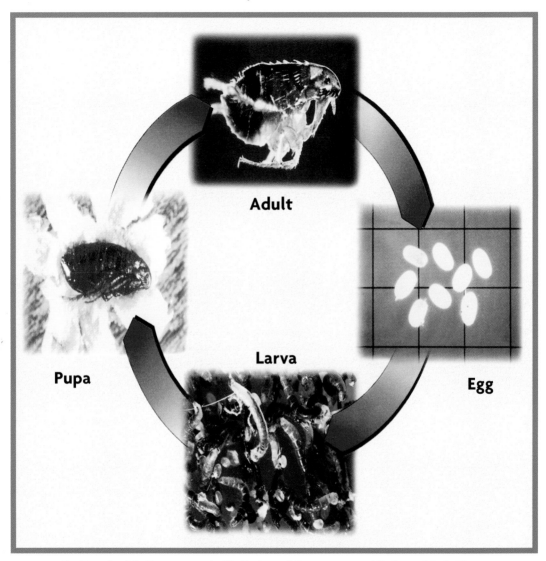

Adult

Larva

Pupa

Egg

The life cycle of the flea was posterised by Fleabusters®. Poster courtesy of Fleabusters®, R_x for Fleas.

cycle and this is why the majority of flea-control products concentrate on this stage. The fact is that adult fleas account for only 1% of the total flea population, and the other 99% exist in pre-adult stages, i.e., eggs, larvae and pupae. The pre-adult stages are barely visible to the naked eye.

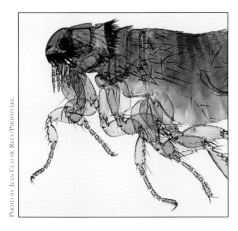

PHOTO BY JEAN CLAUDE REVY/PHOTOTAKE.

THE LIFE CYCLE OF THE FLEA

Eggs are laid on the dog, usually in quantities of about 20 or 30, several times a day. The female adult flea must have a blood meal before each egg-laying session. When first laid, the eggs will cling to the dog's fur, as the eggs are still moist. However, they will quickly dry out and fall from the dog, especially if the dog moves around or scratches. Many eggs will fall off in the dog's favourite area or an area in which

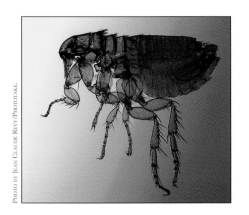

PHOTO BY JEAN CLAUDE REVY/PHOTOTAKE.

On Guard: Catching Fleas Off Guard

Consider the following ways to arm yourself against fleas:
• Add a small amount of pennyroyal or eucalyptus oil to your dog's bath. These natural remedies repel fleas.
• Supplement your dog's food with fresh garlic (minced or grated) and a hearty amount of brewer's yeast, both of which ward off fleas.
• Use a flea comb on your dog daily. Submerge fleas in a cup of bleach to kill them quickly.
• Confine the dog to only a few rooms to limit the spread of fleas in the home.
• Vacuum daily...and get all of the crevices! Dispose of the bag every few days until the problem is under control.
• Wash your dog's bedding daily. Cover cushions where your dog sleeps with towels, and wash the towels often.

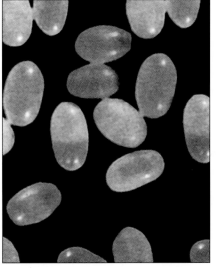

A male dog flea, *Ctenocephalides canis*.

The eggs of the dog flea.

Male cat fleas, *Ctenocephalides felis*, are very commonly found on dogs.

he spends a lot of time, such as his bed.

Once the eggs fall from the dog onto the carpet or furniture, they will hatch into larvae. This takes from one to ten days. Larvae are not particularly mobile, and will usually travel only a few inches from where they hatch. However, they do have a tendency to move away from light and heavy traffic—under furniture and behind doors are common places to find high quantities of flea larvae.

The flea larvae feed on dead organic matter, including adult flea faeces, until they are ready to change into adult fleas. Fleas will usually remain as larvae for around seven days. After this period, the larvae will pupate into protective pupae. While inside the pupae, the larvae will undergo metamorphosis and change into

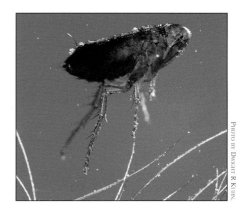

Photo by Dwight R Kuhn.

adult fleas. This can take as little time as a few days, but the adult fleas can remain inside the pupae waiting to hatch for up to two years. The pupae are signalled to hatch by certain stimuli, such as physical pressure—the pupae's being stepped on, heat from an animal lying on the pupae or increased carbon dioxide levels and vibrations—indicating that a suitable host is available.

Once hatched, the adult flea must feed within a few days. Once the adult flea finds a host, it will not leave voluntarily. It only becomes dislodged by grooming or the host animal's scratching. The adult flea will remain on the host for the duration of its life unless forcibly removed.

TREATING THE ENVIRONMENT AND THE DOG

Treating fleas should be a two-pronged attack. First, the environment needs to be treated; this includes carpets and furniture,

Photo by Dwight R Kuhn.

especially the dog's bedding and areas underneath furniture. The environment should be treated with a household spray containing an Insect Growth Regulator (IGR) and an insecticide to kill the adult fleas. Most IGRs are effective against eggs and larvae; they actually mimic the fleas' own hormones and stop the eggs and larvae from developing into adult fleas. There are currently no treatments available to attack the pupa stage of the life cycle, so the adult insecticide is used to kill the newly hatched adult fleas before they find a host. Most IGRs are active for many months, whilst adult insecticides are only active for a few days.

When treating with a household spray, it is a good idea to vacuum before applying the product. This stimulates as many pupae as possible to hatch into adult fleas. The vacuum cleaner should also be treated with a flea treatment to prevent the eggs and larvae that have been hoovered into the vacuum bag from hatching.

The second stage of treatment is to apply an adult insecticide to the dog. Traditionally, this would be in the form of a collar or a spray, but more recent innovations include digestible insecticides that poison the fleas when they ingest the dog's blood. Alternatively, there are drops that, when placed on the back of the animal's neck, spread throughout the fur and skin to kill adult fleas.

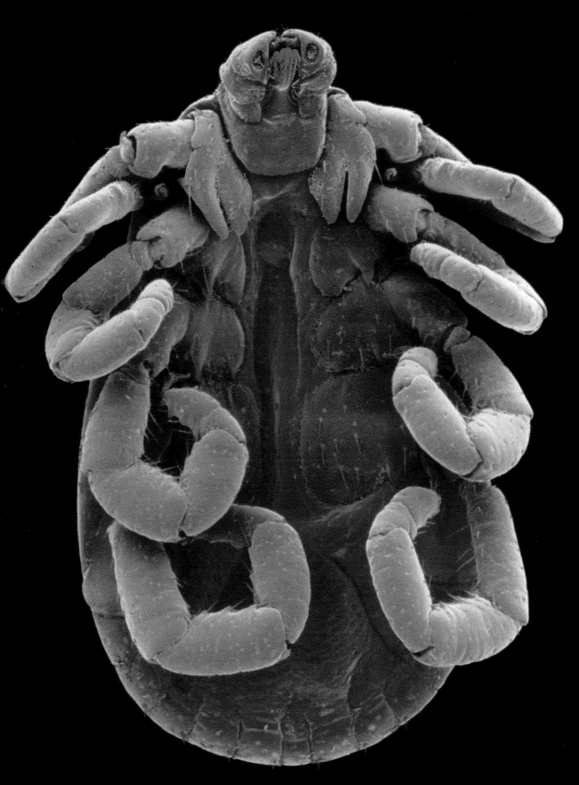

TICKS AND MITES

Though not as common as fleas, ticks and mites are found all over the tropical and temperate world. They don't bite, like fleas; they harpoon. They dig their sharp proboscis (nose) into the dog's skin and drink the blood. Their only food and drink is dog's blood. Dogs can get Lyme disease, Rocky Mountain spotted fever (normally found in the USA only), paralysis and many other diseases from ticks and mites. They may live where fleas are found and they like to hide in cracks or seams in walls wherever dogs live. They are controlled the same way fleas are controlled.

The dog tick, *Dermacentor variabilis*, may well be the most common dog tick in many geographical areas, especially those areas where the climate is hot and humid.

PHOTO BY JEAN CLAUDE REVY/PHOTOTAKE

An uncommon dog tick of the genus *Ixode*. Magnified 10x.

Opposite page: The dog tick, *Dermacentor variabilis*, is probably the most common tick found on dogs. Look at the strength in its eight legs! No wonder it's hard to detach them.

Most dog ticks have life expectancies of a week to six months, depending upon climatic conditions. They can neither jump nor fly, but they can crawl slowly and can range up to 5 metres (16 feet) to reach a sleeping or unsuspecting dog.

MANGE

Mites cause a skin irritation called mange. Some are contagious, like *Cheyletiella*, ear mites, scabies and chiggers. The non-contagious mites are *Demodex*. Mites that cause ear-mite infestation are usually controlled with ivermectin, which is often toxic to Collies and probably should be avoided in all herding breeds.

It is essential that your dog be treated for mange as quickly as possible because some forms of mange are transmissible to people.

A brown dog tick, *Rhipicephalus sanguineus*, is an uncommon but annoying tick found on dogs.

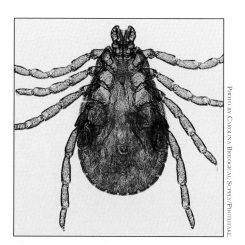

PHOTO BY CAROLINA BIOLOGICAL SUPPLY/PHOTOTAKE.

Neapolitan Mastiff

Two views of the mange mite, *Psoroptes bovis*.

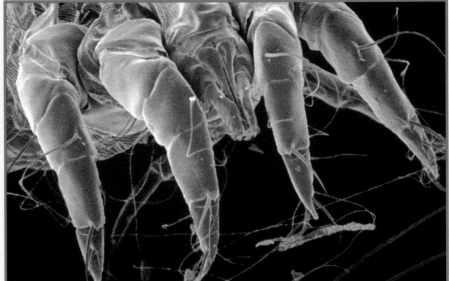

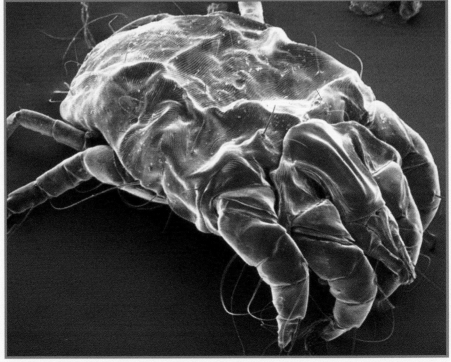

INTERNAL PARASITES

Most animals—fishes, birds and mammals, including dogs and humans—have worms and other parasites that live inside their bodies. According to Dr Herbert R Axelrod, the fish pathologist, there are two kinds of parasites: dumb and smart. The smart parasites live in peaceful cooperation with their hosts (symbiosis), while the dumb parasites kill their host. Most of the worm infections are relatively easy to control. If they are not controlled they eventually weaken the host dog to the point that other medical problems occur, but they are not dumb parasites.

ROUNDWORMS

The roundworms that infect dogs are scientifically known as *Toxocara canis*. They live in the dog's intestines. The worms shed eggs continually. It has been estimated that a dog produces about 150 grammes of faeces every day. Each gramme of faeces averages 10,000–12,000 eggs of roundworms. There are no known areas in which dogs roam that do not contain roundworm eggs. The greatest danger of roundworms is

Did You Know?

Ridding your puppy of worms is VERY IMPORTANT because certain worms that puppies carry, such as tapeworms and roundworms, can infect humans.

Breeders initiate a deworming programme at or about four weeks of age. The routine is repeated every two or three weeks until the puppy is three months old. The breeder from whom you obtained your puppy should provide you with the complete details of the deworming programme.

Your veterinary surgeon can prescribe and monitor the programme of deworming for you. The usual programme is treating the puppy every 15–20 days until the puppy is positively worm free.

It is advised that you only treat your puppy with drugs that are recommended professionally.

The roundworm, *Rhabditis*. The roundworm can infect both dogs and humans.

127

The roundworm *Rhabditis*.

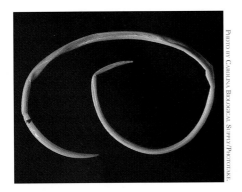

PHOTO BY CAROLINA BIOLOGICAL SUPPLY/PHOTOTAKE

PHOTO BY DWIGHT R KUHN.

Male and female hookworms, *Ancylostoma caninum*, are uncommonly found in pet or show dogs in Britain. Hookworms may infect other dogs that have exposure to grasslands.

that they infect people too! It is wise to have your dog tested regularly for roundworms.

Pigs also have roundworm infections that can be passed to humans and dogs. The typical roundworm parasite is called *Ascaris lumbricoides*.

HOOKWORMS
The worm *Ancylostoma caninum* is commonly called the dog hookworm. It is dangerous to humans and cats. It also has teeth

by which it attaches itself to the intestines of the dog. It changes the site of its attachment about six times a day and the dog loses blood from each detachment, possibly causing iron-deficiency anaemia. Hookworms are easily purged from the dog with many medications. Milbemycin oxime, which also serves as a heartworm preventative in Collies, can be used for this purpose.

In Britain the 'temperate climate' hookworm (*Uncinaria stenocephala*) is rarely found in pet or show dogs, but can occur in hunting packs, racing Greyhounds and sheepdogs because the worms can be prevalent wherever dogs are exercised regularly on grassland.

Did You Know?

Caring for the puppy starts before the puppy is born by keeping the dam healthy and well-nourished. Most puppies have worms, even if they are not evident, so a worming programme is essential. The worms continually shed eggs except during their dormant stage, when they just rest in the tissues of the puppy. During this stage they are not evident during a routine examination.

Did You Know?

Average size dogs can pass 1,360,000 roundworm eggs every day.

For example, if there were only 1 million dogs in the world, the world would be saturated with 1,300 metric tonnes of dog faeces.

These faeces would contain 15,000,000,000 roundworm eggs.

7–31% of home gardens and children's play boxes in the U. S. contain roundworm eggs.

Flushing dog's faeces down the toilet is not a safe practice because the usual sewage treatments do not destroy roundworm eggs.

Infected puppies start shedding roundworm eggs at 3 weeks of age. They can be infected by their mother's milk.

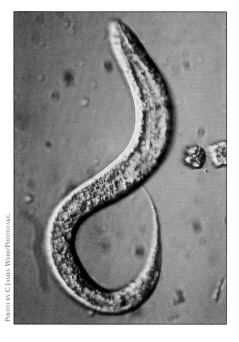

The infective stage of the hookworm larva.

PHOTO BY C JAMES WEBB/PHOTOTAKE.

TAPEWORMS

There are many species of tapeworms. They are carried by fleas! The dog eats the flea and starts the tapeworm cycle. Humans can also be infected with tapeworms, so don't eat fleas! Fleas are so small that your dog could pass them onto your hands, your plate or your food and thus make it possible for you to ingest a flea which is carrying tapeworm eggs.

While tapeworm infection is not life threatening in dogs (smart parasite!), it can be the cause of a very serious liver disease for humans. About 50 percent of the humans infected with

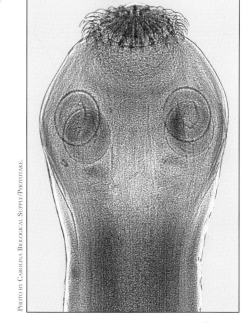

The head and rostellum (the round prominence on the scolex) of a tapeworm, which infects dogs and humans.

PHOTO BY CAROLINA BIOLOGICAL SUPPLY/PHOTOTAKE.

Echinococcus multilocularis, a type of tapeworm that causes alveolar hydatis, perish.

HEARTWORMS

Heartworms are thin, extended worms up to 30 cms (12 ins) long which live in a dog's heart and the major blood vessels surrounding it. Dogs may have up to 200 of these worms. The symptoms may be loss of energy, loss of appetite, coughing, the development of a pot belly and anaemia.

Heartworms are transmitted by mosquitoes. The mosquito drinks the blood of an infected dog and takes in larvae with the blood. The larvae, called microfilaria, develop within the body of the mosquito and are passed on to the next dog bitten after the larvae mature. It takes two to three weeks for the larvae to develop to the infective stage within the body of the mosquito. Dogs should be treated at about six weeks of age, then every six months.

Did You Know?

Humans, rats, squirrels, foxes, coyotes, wolves, mixed breeds of dogs and purebred dogs are all susceptible to tapeworm infection. Except in humans, tapeworms are usually not a fatal infection.

Infected individuals can harbour a thousand parasitic worms.

Tapeworms have two sexes—male and female (many other worms have only one sex—male and female in the same worm).

If dogs eat infected rats or mice, they get the tapeworm disease.

One month after attaching to a dog's intestine, the worm starts shedding eggs. These eggs are infective immediately.

Infective eggs can live for a few months without a host animal.

Roundworms, whipworms and tapeworms are just a few of the other commonly known worms that infect dogs.

Blood testing for heartworms is not necessarily indicative of how seriously your dog is infected. This is a dangerous disease. Although heartworm is a problem for dogs in America, Australia, Asia and Central Europe, dogs in the United Kingdom are not affected by heartworm.

The heartworm, *Dirofilaria immitis*.

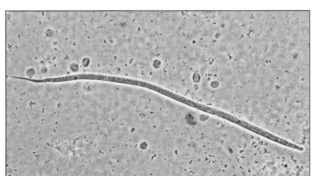

PHOTO BY JAMES E HAYDEN, RPB/PHOTOTAKE

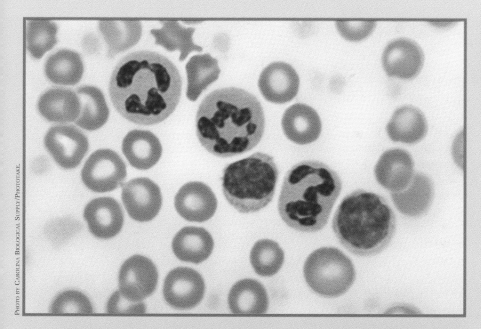

Magnified heartworm larvae, *Dirofilaria immitis.*

PHOTO BY CAROLINA BIOLOGICAL SUPPLY/PHOTOTAKE.

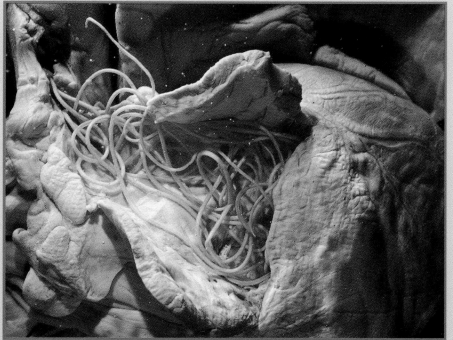

The heart of a dog infected with canine heartworm, *Dirofilaria immitis.*

PHOTO BY JAMES E HAYDEN, RPB/PHOTOTAKE.

Neapolitan Mastiffs are prone to eye abnormalities. You should consult a veterinary ophthalmologist when you notice the early signs of any eye problems. This Neo suffers from a prominent lower central ectropion, with a medial and lateral entropion (known as 'diamond-eye' syndrome, which is common in giant breeds). There is also some other source of irritation in the left eye.

Lower entropion, or rolling in of the eyelid, is causing irritation in the left eye of this young dog. Several extra eyelashes, or distichiasis, are present on the upper lid.

A PET OWNER'S GUIDE TO COMMON OPHTHALMIC DISEASES
by Prof. Dr Robert L Peiffer, Jr.

Few would argue that vision is the most important of the cognitive senses, and maintenance of a normal visual system is important for an optimal quality of life. Likewise, pet owners tend to be acutely aware of their pet's eyes and vision, which is important because early detection of ocular disease will optimize therapeutic outcomes. The eye is a sensitive organ with minimal reparative capabilities, and with some diseases, such as glaucoma, uveitis and retinal detachment, delay in diagnosis and treatment can be critical in terms of whether vision can be preserved.

The causes of ocular disease are quite varied; the nature of dogs make them susceptible to traumatic conditions, the most common of which include proptosis of the globe, cat scratch injuries and penetrating wounds from foreign objects, including sticks and air rifle pellets. Infectious diseases caused by bacteria, viruses or fungi may be localized to the eye or part of a systemic infection. Many of the common conditions, including eyelid conformational problems, cataracts, glaucoma and retinal degenerations have a genetic basis.

Before acquiring your puppy it is important to ascertain that both parents have been examined and certified free of eye disease by a veterinary ophthalmologist. Since many of these genetic diseases can be detected early in life, acquire the pup with the condition that it pass a thorough ophthalmic examination by a qualified specialist.

LID CONFORMATIONAL ABNORMALITIES
Rolling in (entropion) or out (ectropion) of the lids tends to be a breed-related problem. Entropion can involve the upper and/or lower lids. Signs usually appear between 3 and 12 months of age. The irritation caused by the eyelid hairs rubbing on the surface of the

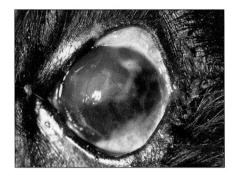

cornea may result in blinking, tearing and damage to the cornea. Ectropion is likewise breed-related and is considered 'normal' in hounds, for instance; unlike entropion, which results in acute discomfort, ectropion may cause chronic irritation related to exposure and the pooling of secretions. Most of these cases can be managed medically with daily irrigation with sterile saline and topical antibiotics when required.

EYELASH ABNORMALITIES

Dogs normally have lashes only on the upper lids, in contrast to humans. Occasionally, extra eyelashes may be seen emerging at the eyelid margin (distichiasis) or through the inner surface of the eyelid (ectopic cilia).

CONJUNCTIVITIS

Inflammation of the conjunctiva, the pink tissue that lines the lids and the anterior portion of the sclera, is generally accompanied by redness, discharge and mild discomfort. The majority of cases are either associated with bacterial infections or dry eye syndrome. Fortunately, topical medications are generally effective in curing or controlling the problem.

DRY EYE SYNDROME

Dry eye syndrome (keratoconjunctivitis sicca) is a common cause of external ocular disease. Discharge is typically thick and sticky, and keratitis is a frequent component; any breed can be affected. While some cases can be associated with toxic effects of drugs, including the sulfa antibiotics, the cause in the majority of the cases cannot be determined and is assumed to be immune-mediated.

Keratoconjunctivitis sicca, seen here in the right eye of a middle-aged dog, causes a characteristic thick mucous discharge as well as secondary corneal changes.

Left: Prolapse of the gland of the third eyelid in the right eye of a pup. Right: In this case, in the right eye of a young dog, the prolapsed gland can be seen emerging between the edge of the third eyelid and the corneal surface.

133

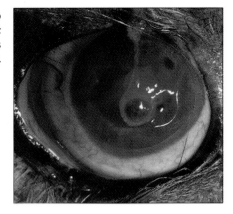

Multiple deep ulcerations affect the cornea of this middle-aged dog.

PROLAPSE OF THE GLAND OF THE THIRD EYELID

In this condition, commonly referred to as *cherry eye*, the gland of the third eyelid, which produces about one-third of the aqueous phase of the tear film and is normally situated within the anterior orbit, prolapses to emerge as a pink fleshy mass protruding over the edge of the third eyelid, between the third eyelid and the cornea. The condition usually develops during the first year of life and, while mild irritation may result, the condition is unsightly as much as anything else.

Lipid deposition can occur as a primary inherited dystrophy, or secondarily to hypercholesterolemia (in dogs frequently associated with hypothyroidism), chronic corneal inflammation or neoplasia. The deposits in this dog assume an oval pattern in the centre of the cornea.

CORNEAL DISEASE

The cornea is the clear front part of the eye that provides the first step in the collection of light on its journey to be eventually focused onto the retina, and most corneal diseases will be manifested by alterations in corneal transparency. The cornea is an exquisitely innervated tissue, and defects in corneal integrity are accompanied by pain, which is demonstrated by squinting.

Corneal ulcers may occur secondary to trauma or to irritation from entropion or ectopic cilia. In middle-aged or older dogs, epithelial ulcerations may occur spontaneously due to an inherent defect; these are referred to as indolent or Boxer ulcers, in recognition of the breed in which we see the condition most frequently. Infection may occur secondarily. Ulcers can be potentially blinding conditions; severity is dependent upon the size and depth of the ulcer and other complicating features.

Non-ulcerative keratitis tends to have an immune-mediated component and is managed by topical immunosuppressants, usually corticosteroids. Corneal edema can occur in elderly dogs. It is due to a failure of the corneal endothelial 'pump.'

The cornea responds to chronic irritation by transforming into skin-like tissue that is evident clinically

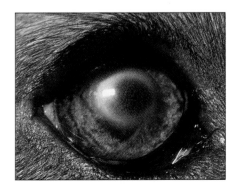

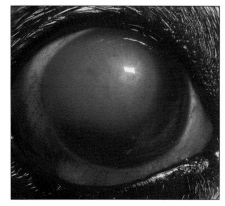

by pigmentation, scarring and vascularization; some cases may respond to tear stimulants, lubricants and topical corticosteroids, while others benefit from surgical narrowing of the eyelid opening in order to enhance corneal protection.

UVEITIS
Inflammation of the vascular tissue of the eye–the uvea—is a common and potentially serious disease in dogs. While it may occur secondarily to trauma or other intraocular diseases, such as

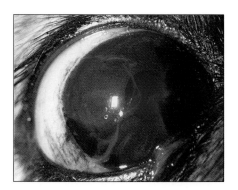

cataracts, most commonly uveitis is associated with some type of systemic infectious or neoplastic process. Uncontrolled, uveitis can lead to blinding cataracts, glaucoma and/or retinal detachments, and aggressive symptomatic therapy with dilating agents (to prevent pupillary adhesions) and anti-inflammatories are critical.

GLAUCOMA
The eye is essentially a hollow fluid-filled sphere, and the pressure within is maintained by regulation of the rate of fluid production and fluid egress at 10–20 mms of mercury. The retinal cells are extremely sensitive to elevations of intraocular pressure and, unless controlled, permanent blindness can occur within hours to days. In acute glaucoma, the conjunctiva becomes congested, the cornea cloudy, the pupil moderate and fixed; the eye is generally painful and avisual. Increased constant signs of discom-

Corneal edema can develop as a slowly progressive process in elderly Boston Terriers, Miniature Dachshunds and Miniature Poodles, as well as others, as a result of the inability of the corneal endothelial 'pump' to maintain a state of dehydration.

Medial pigmentary keratitis in this dog is associated with irritation from prominent facial folds.

135

Glaucoma in the dog most commonly occurs as a sudden extreme elevation of intraocular pressure, frequently to three to four times the norm. The eye of this dog demonstrates the common signs of episcleral injection, or redness; mild diffuse corneal cloudiness, due to edema; and a mid-sized fixed pupil.

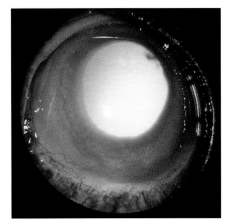

Left: The typical posterior subcapsular cataract appears between one and two years of age, but rarely progresses to where the animal has visual problems. Right: Inherited cataracts generally appear between three and six years of age, and progress to the stage seen where functional vision is significantly impaired.

fort will accompany chronic cases.

Management of glaucoma is one of the most challenging situations the veterinary ophthalmologist faces; in spite of intense efforts, many of these cases will result in blindness.

CATARACTS AND LENS DISLOCATION

Cataracts are the most common blinding condition in dogs; fortunately, they are readily amenable to surgical intervention, with excellent results in terms of restoration of vision and replacement of the cataractous lens with a synthetic one. Most cataracts in dogs are inherited; less commonly cataracts can be secondary to trauma, other ocular diseases, including uveitis, glaucoma, lens luxation and retinal degeneration, or secondary to an underlying systemic metabolic disease, including diabetes and Cushing's disease. Signs include a progressive loss of the bright dark appearance of the pupil, which is replaced by a blue-grey hazy appearance. In this respect, cataracts need to be distinguished from the normal ageing process of nuclear sclerosis, which occurs in middle-aged or older animals, and has minimal effect on vision.

Lens dislocation occurs in dogs and frequently leads to secondary glaucoma; early removal of the dislocated lens is generally curative.

RETINAL DISEASE

Retinal degenerations are usually inherited, but may be associated with vitamin E deficiency in dogs. While signs are variable, most

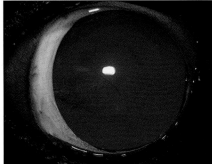

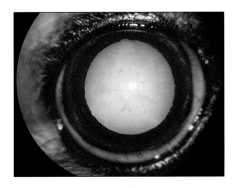

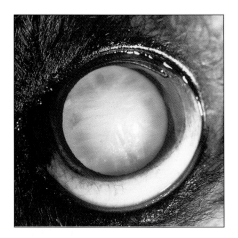

frequently one notes a decrease in vision over a period of months, which typically starts out as a night blindness. The cause of a more rapid loss of vision due to retinal degeneration occurs over days to weeks is labeled sudden acquired retinal degeneration or SARD; the outcome, however, is unfortunately usually similar to inherited and nutritional conditions, as the

retinal tissues possess minimal regenerative capabilities. Most pets, however, with a bit of extra care and attention, show an amazing ability to adapt to an avisual world, and can be maintained as pets with a satisfactory quality of life.

Detachment of the retina—due to accumulation of blood between the retina and the underling uvea, which is called the *choroid*—can occur secondarily to retinal tears or holes, tractional forces within the eye, or as a result of uveitis. These types of detachments may be amenable to surgical repair if diagnosed early.

OPTIC NERVE

Optic neuritis, or inflammation of the nerve that connects the eye with the brain stem, is a relatively uncommon condition that presents usually with rather sudden loss of vision and widely dilated non-responsive pupils.

Anterior lens luxation can occur as a primary disease in the terrier breeds, or secondarily to trauma. The fibres that hold the lens in place rupture and the lens may migrate through the pupil to be situated in front of the iris. Secondary glaucoma is a frequent and significant complication that can be avoided if the dislocated lens is removed surgically.

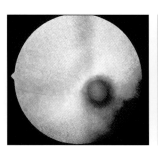
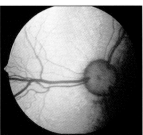
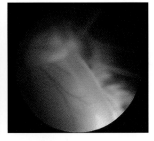

Left: The posterior pole of a normal fundus is shown; prominent are the head of the optic nerve and the retinal blood vessels. The retina is transparent, and the prominent green tapetum is seen superiorly.
Centre: An eye with inherited retinal dysplasia is depicted. The tapetal retina superior to the optic disc is disorganised, with multifocal areas of hyperplasia of the retinal pigment epithelium.
Right: Severe collie eye anomaly and a retinal detachment; this eye is unfortunately blind.

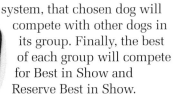

When you purchased your Neapolitan Mastiff you should have made it clear to the breeder whether you wanted one just as a loveable companion and pet, or if you hoped to be buying a Neapolitan Mastiff with show prospects. No reputable breeder would have sold you a young puppy saying that it was definitely of show quality, for so much can go wrong during the early weeks and months of a puppy's development. If you plan to show, what you will hopefully have acquired is a puppy with 'show potential.'

Exhibiting a Neapolitan Mastiff in the show ring may look easy to a novice, but it usually takes a lot of hard work and devotion to do top winning at a show such as the prestigious World Dog Show, not to mention a little luck too!

The first concept that the canine novice learns when watching a dog show is that each dog first competes against members of its own breed. Once the judge has selected the best member of each breed, provided that the show is judged on a Group

system, that chosen dog will compete with other dogs in its group. Finally, the best of each group will compete for Best in Show and Reserve Best in Show.

The second concept that you must understand is that the dogs are not actually competing against one another. The judge compares

Did You Know?

You can get information about dog shows from kennel clubs and breed clubs:

Fédération Cynologique Internationale
14, rue Leopold II, B-6530 Thuin, Belgium
www.fci.be

The Kennel Club
1-5 Clarges St., Piccadilly, London W1Y 8AB, UK
www.the-kennel-club.org.uk

American Kennel Club
5580 Centerview Dr., Raleigh, NC 27606-3390, USA
www.akc.org

Canadian Kennel Club
89 Skyway Ave., Suite 100, Etobicoke, Ontario
M9W 6R4 Canada
www.ckc.ca

These clubs often host both Championship and Open shows, and sometimes Match meetings and Special Events, all of which could be of interest, even if you are only an onlooker. Clubs also send out newsletters and some organise training days and seminars in order that people may learn more about their chosen breed. To locate the nearest breed club for you, contact The Kennel Club, the ruling body for the British dog world. The Kennel Club governs not only conformation shows but also working trials, obedience trials, agility trials and field trials. The Kennel Club furnishes the rules and regulations for all these events

each dog against the breed standard, which is a written description of the ideal specimen of the breed. Whilst some early breed standards were indeed based on specific dogs that were famous or popular, many dedicated enthusiasts say that a perfect specimen, described in the standard, has never been bred. Thus the 'perfect' dog never walked into a show ring, has never been bred and, to the woe of dog breeders around the globe, does not exist. Breeders attempt to get as close to this ideal as possible with every litter, but theoretically the 'perfect' dog is so elusive that it is impossible (and if the 'perfect' dog were born, breeders and judges would never agree that it was indeed 'perfect').

If you are interested in exploring dog shows, your best bet is to join your local breed club.

plus general dog registration and other basic requirements of dog ownership. Its annual show, called the Crufts Dog Show, held in Birmingham, is the largest bench show in England. Every year around 20,000 of the U.K.'s best dogs qualify to participate in this marvellous show, which lasts four days.

The Kennel Club governs many different kinds of shows in Great Britain, Australia, South Africa and beyond. At the most competitive and prestigious of these shows, the Championship Shows, a dog can earn Challenge Certificates and thereby become a Show Champion or a Champion. A dog must earn three Challenge Certificates under three different judges to earn the prefix of 'Sh

Ch' or 'Ch.' Note that some breeds must also qualify in a field trial in order to gain the title of full champion. Challenge Certificates are awarded to a very small percentage of the dogs competing, especially as dogs which are already Champions compete with others for these coveted CCs. The number of Challenge Certificates awarded in any one year is based upon the total number of dogs in each breed entered for competition. There are three types of Championship Shows: an all-breed General Championship show for all-Kennel-Club recognised breeds; a Group Championship Show, limited to breeds within one of the Groups; and a Breed Show, usually confined to a single breed. The Kennel Club determines which breeds at which Championship Shows will have the opportunity to earn Challenge Certificates (or tickets). Serious exhibitors often will opt not to participate if the tickets are withheld at a particular show. This policy makes earning championships ever more difficult to accomplish.

Open Shows are generally less competitive and are frequently used as 'practice shows' for young dogs. There are hundreds of Open Shows each year that can be invitingly social events and are great first show experiences for the novice. Even if you're considering just watching a show to wet

Did You Know?

The FCI *does not* issue pedigrees. The FCI members and contract partners are responsible for issuing pedigrees and training judges in their own countries. The FCI does maintain a list of judges and makes sure that they are recognised throughout the FCI member countries.

The FCI also *does not* act as a breeder referral; breeder information is available from FCI-recognised national canine societies in each of the FCI's member countries.

your paws, an Open Show is a great choice.

Whilst Championship and Open Shows are most important for the beginner to understand, there are other types of shows in which the interested dog owner can participate. Training clubs sponsor Matches that can be entered on the day of the show for a nominal fee. In these introductory-level exhibitions, two dogs are pulled out of a hat and 'matched,' the winner of that match goes on to the next round, and eventually only one dog is left undefeated.

Exemption Shows are much more light-hearted affairs with usually only four pedigree classes and several 'fun' classes, all of which can be entered on the day. The proceeds of an Exemption Show must be given to a charity and are sometimes held in conjunction with small agricultural shows. Limited Shows are also available in small number, but entry is restricted to members of the club which hosts the show, although one can usually join the club when making an entry.

Before you actually step into the ring, you would be well advised to sit back and observe the judge's ring procedure. If it is your first time in the ring, do not be over-anxious and run to the front of the line. It is much better to stand back and study how the exhibitor in front of you is

If your Neapolitan Mastiff is of show quality, you may want to give conformation showing a try.

performing. The judge asks each handler to 'stand' the dog, hopefully showing the dog off to his best advantage. The judge will observe the dog from a distance and from different angles, approach the dog, check his teeth, overall structure, alertness and muscle tone, as well as consider how well the dog 'conforms' to the standard. Most importantly, the judge will have the exhibitor move the dog around the ring in some pattern that he or she should specify (another advantage to not going first, but always listen since some judges change their directions, and the judge is always right!). Finally the judge will give the dog one last look before moving on to the next exhibitor.

If you are not in the top three at your first show, do not be discouraged. Be patient and consistent and you may eventually find yourself in the winning lineup. Remember that the winners were once in your shoes and have devoted many hours and much money to earn the placement. If you find that your dog is losing every time and never getting a nod, it may be time to consider a different dog sport or just enjoy your Neapolitan Mastiff as a pet.

WORKING TRIALS

Working trials can be entered by any well-trained dog of any breed, not just Gundogs or Working dogs. Many dogs that earn the Kennel Club Good Citizen Dog award choose to participate in a working trial. There are five stakes at both open and championship levels: Companion Dog (CD), Utility Dog (UD), Working Dog (WD), Tracking Dog (TD) and Patrol Dog (PD). As in conformation shows, dogs

Classes at Dog Shows

There can be as many as 18 classes per sex for your breed. Check the show schedule carefully to make sure that you have entered your dog in the appropriate class. Among the classes offered can be: Beginners; Minor Puppy (ages 6 to 9 months); Puppy (ages 6 to 12 months); Junior (ages 6 to 18 months); Beginners (handler or dog never won first place) as well as the following, each of which is defined in the schedule: Maiden; Novice; Tyro; Debutant; Undergraduate; Graduate; Postgraduate; Minor Limit; Mid Limit; Limit; Open; Veteran; Stud Dog; Brood Bitch; Progeny; Brace and Team.

compete against a standard and if the dog reaches the qualifying mark, it obtains a certificate. Divided into groups, each exercise must be achieved 70 percent in order to qualify. If the dog achieves 80 percent in the open level, it receives a Certificate of Merit (COM); in the championship level, it receives a Qualifying Certificate. At the CD stake, dogs must participate in four groups: Control, Stay, Agility and Search (Retrieve and Nosework). At the next three levels, UD, WD and TD, there are only three groups: Control, Agility and Nosework.

Agility consists of three jumps: a vertical scale up a wall of planks; a clear jump over a basic hurdle with a removable top bar; and a long jump across angled planks.

To earn the UD, WD and TD, dogs must track approximately one-half mile for articles laid from one-half hour to three hours ago. Tracks consist of turns and legs, and fresh ground is used for each participant.

The fifth stake, PD, involves teaching manwork, which is not recommended for every breed.

FIELD TRIALS AND WORKING TESTS

Working tests are frequently used to prepare dogs for field trials, the purpose of which is to heighten the instincts and natural abilities of gundogs. Live game is not used in working tests. Unlike field trials, working tests do not count toward a dog's record at The Kennel Club, though the same judges often oversee working tests. Field trials began in England in 1947 and are only moderately popular amongst dog folk. Whilst breeders of Working and Gundog breeds concern themselves with the field abilities of their dogs, there is considerably less interest in field trials than dog shows. In order for dogs to become full champions, certain breeds must qualify in the field as well. Upon gaining three CCs in the show ring, the dog is designated a Show Champion (Sh Ch). The title Champion (Ch) requires that the dog gain an award at a field trial, be a 'special qualifier' at a field trial or pass a 'special show dog qualifier' judged by a field trial judge on a shooting day.

FÉDÉRATION CYNOLOGIQUE INTERNATIONALE

Established in 1911, the Fédération Cynologique Internationale (FCI) represents the 'world kennel club.' This international body brings uniformity to the breeding, judging and showing of purebred dogs. Although the FCI originally included only four European nations: France, Holland, Austria and Belgium (which remains its headquarters), the organisation today embraces nations on six

Neapolitan Mastiffs being judged in the Brace Class at an international championship show. Notice that two handlers were needed (usually only one handler escorts the brace).

continents and recognises well over 300 breeds of purebred dog. There are three titles attainable through the FCI: the International Champion, which is the most prestigious; the International Beauty Champion, which is based on aptitude certificates in different countries; and the International Trial Champion, which is based on achievement in obedience trials in different countries. Quarantine laws in England and Australia prohibit most of their exhibitors from entering FCI shows. The rest of the Continent does participate in these impressive canine spectacles, the largest of which is the World Dog Show, hosted in a different country each year. FCI sponsors both national and international shows. The hosting country determines the judging system and breed standards are always based on the breed's country of origin.

As a Neapolitan Mastiff owner, you selected your dog so that you and your loved ones could have a companion, a protector, a friend and a four-legged family member. You invest time, money and effort to care for and train the family's new charge. Of course, this chosen canine behaves perfectly! Well, perfectly like a dog. When discussing the Neapolitan Mastiff, owners have much to consider.

THINK LIKE A DOG

Dogs do not think like humans, nor do humans think like dogs, though we try. Unfortunately, a dog is incapable of figuring out how humans think, so the responsibility falls on the owner to adopt a proper canine mindset. Dogs cannot rationalise, and dogs exist in the present moment. Many dog owners make the mistake in training of thinking that they can reprimand their dog for something he did a while ago. Basically, you cannot even reprimand a dog for something he did 20 seconds ago! Either catch him in the act or forget it! It is a waste of your and your dog's time—in his mind, you are reprimanding him for whatever he is doing at that moment.

The following behavioural problems represent some which owners most commonly encounter. Every dog is unique and every situation is unique. No author could purport to solve your Neapolitan Mastiff's problem simply by reading a script. Here we outline some basic 'dogspeak' so that owners' chances of solving behavioural problems are increased. Discuss bad habits with your veterinary surgeon and he/she can recommend a behavioural specialist to consult in appropriate cases. Since behavioural abnormalities are the leading reason owners abandon their pets, we hope that you will make a valiant effort to solve your Neapolitan Mastiff's problem. Patience and understanding are virtues that dwell in every pet-loving household.

Did You Know?

Never scream, shout, jump or run about if you want your dog to stay calm. You set the example for your dog's behaviour in most circumstances. Learn from your dog's reaction to your behaviour and act accordingly.

AGGRESSION

Aggression is a problem that concerns owners of all dogs, and Neapolitan Mastiffs are no exception. Aggression can be a very big problem in dogs, even more so in a very large breed like the Neapolitan. Aggression, when not controlled, always becomes dangerous. An aggressive dog, no matter the size, may lunge at, bite or even attack a person or another dog. Aggressive behaviour is not to be tolerated. It is more than just inappropriate behaviour; it is not safe, especially with a large breed such as the Neapolitan Mastiff. It is painful for a family to watch their dog become unpredictable in his behaviour to the point where they are afraid of him. Whilst not all aggressive behaviour is dangerous, growling, baring teeth, etc., can be frightening. It is important to ascertain why the dog is acting in this manner. Aggression is a display of dominance, and the dog should not have the dominant role in its pack, which is, in this case, your family.

It is important not to challenge an aggressive dog as this could provoke an attack. Observe your Neapolitan Mastiff's body language. Does he make direct eye contact and stare? Does he try to make himself as large as possible: ears pricked, chest out, tail erect? Height and size signify authority in a dog pack—being

'My back doesn't itch...I want my belly scratched.' Being able to read doggie language comes from experience.

taller or 'above' another dog literally means that he is 'above' in the social status. These body signals tell you that your Neapolitan Mastiff thinks he is in charge, a problem that needs to be addressed. An aggressive dog is unpredictable: you never know when he is going to strike and what he is going to do. You cannot understand why a dog that is playful and loving one minute is growling and snapping the next.

The best solution is to consult a behavioural specialist, one who

Did You Know?

Physical games like pulling contests, wrestling, jumping and teasing should not be encouraged. Inciting the dog's crazy behaviour tends to confuse a dog. The owner has to be able to control his dog at all times; your dog has to know that you're the leader and that he should always behave politely, even in play.

has experience with the Neapolitan Mastiff if possible. Together, perhaps you can pinpoint the cause of your dog's aggression and do something about it. An aggressive dog cannot be trusted, and a dog that cannot be trusted is not safe to have as a family pet. If, very unusually, you find that your pet has become untrustworthy and you feel it necessary to seek a new home with a more suitable family and environment, explain fully to the new owners all your reasons for rehoming the dog to be fair to all concerned. In the very worst case, you will have to consider euthanasia.

AGGRESSION TOWARD OTHER DOGS

A dog's aggressive behaviour toward another dog sometimes stems from insufficient exposure to other dogs at an early age. If other dogs make your Neapolitan Mastiff nervous and agitated, he will lash out as a defensive

> **Did You Know?**
>
> Your dog inherited the pack-leader mentality. He only knows about pecking order. He instinctively wants to be top dog but you have to convince him that you are boss. There is no such thing as living in a democracy with your dog. You are the dictator, the absolute monarch.

mechanism, though this behaviour is thankfully uncommon in the breed. A dog who has not received sufficient exposure to other canines tends to believe that he is the only dog on the planet. The animal becomes so dominant that he does not even show signs that he is fearful or threatened. Without growling or any other physical signal as a warning, he will lunge at and bite the other dog. A way to correct this is to let your Neapolitan Mastiff approach another dog when walking on lead. Watch very closely and at the very first sign of aggression, correct your Neapolitan Mastiff and pull him away. Scold him for any sign of discomfort, and then praise him when he ignores or tolerates the other dog. Keep this up until he stops the aggressive behaviour, learns to ignore the other dog or accepts other dogs. Praise him lavishly for his correct behaviour.

> **Did You Know?**
>
> If your dog barks or growls at strangers, or growls at anyone coming near his food while he is eating, playing with a toy or taking a rest in his favourite spot, he needs proper professional training because sooner or later this behaviour can result in someone being bitten.

Did You Know?

Dog aggression is a serious problem. NEVER give an aggressive dog to someone else. The dog will usually be more aggressive in a new situation where his leadership is unchallenged and unquestioned (in his mind).

DOMINANT AGGRESSION

A social hierarchy is firmly established in a wild dog pack. The dog wants to dominate those under him and please those above him. Dogs know that there must be a leader. If you are not the obvious choice for emperor, the dog will assume the throne! These conflicting innate desires are what a dog owner is up against when he sets about training a dog. In training a dog to obey commands, the owner is reinforcing that he is the top dog in the 'pack' and that the dog should, and should want to, serve his superior. Thus, the owner is suppressing the dog's urge to dominate by modifying his behaviour and making him obedient.

An important part of training is taking every opportunity to reinforce that you are the leader. The simple action of making your Neapolitan Mastiff sit to wait for his food says that you control when he eats and that he is dependent on you for food. Although it may be difficult, do

not give in to your dog's wishes every time he whines at you or looks at you with his pleading eyes. It is a constant effort to show the dog that his place in the pack is at the bottom. This is not meant to sound cruel or inhumane. You love your Neapolitan Mastiff and you should treat him with care and affection. You (hopefully) did not

A raised knee is an often-used technique to stop a dog from jumping up. Reinforce the lesson positively by praising the dog when all four paws are on the ground.

Did You Know?

If you are approached by an aggressive, growling dog, do not run away. Simply stand still and avoid eye contact. If you have something in your hand (like a handbag), throw it sideways away from your body to distract the dog from making a frontal attack.

get a dog just so you could boss around another creature. Dog training is not about being cruel or feeling important, it is about moulding the dog's behaviour into what is acceptable and teaching him to live by your rules. In theory, it is quite simple: catch him in appropriate behaviour and reward him for it. Add a dog into the equation and it becomes a bit more trying, but as a rule of thumb, positive reinforcement is what works best.

With a dominant dog, punishment and negative reinforcement can have the opposite effect of what you are after. It can make a dog fearful and/or act out aggressively if he feels he is being challenged. Remember, a dominant dog perceives himself at

Did You Know?

Fear in a grown dog is often the result of improper or incomplete socialisation as a pup, or it can be the result of a traumatic experience he suffered when young. Keep in mind that the term 'traumatic' is relative—something that you would not think twice about can leave a lasting negative impression on a puppy. If the dog experiences a similar experience later in life, he may try to fight back to protect himself. Again, this behaviour is very unpredictable, especially if you do not know what is triggering his fear.

Did You Know?

DANGER! If you and your on-lead dog are approached by a larger, running dog that is not restrained, walk away from the dog as quickly as possible. Don't allow your dog to make eye contact with the other dog. You should not make eye contact either. In dog terms, eye contact indicates a challenge.

the top of the social heap and will fight to defend his perceived status. The best way to prevent that is never to give him reason to think that he is in control in the first place. If you are having trouble training your Neapolitan Mastiff and it seems as if he is constantly challenging your authority, seek the help of an obedience trainer or behavioural specialist. A professional will work with both you and your dog to teach you effective techniques to use at home. Beware of trainers who rely on excessively harsh methods; scolding is necessary now and then, but the focus in your training should always be on positive reinforcement.

If you can isolate what brings out the fear reaction, you can help the dog get over it. Supervise your Neapolitan Mastiff's interactions with people and other dogs, and praise the dog when it goes well. If he starts to act aggressively in a situation, correct him and remove

A male dog uses urination to mark his territory. He recognises his own scent and can smell if another dog has been there.

him from the situation. Do not let people approach the dog and start petting him without your express permission. That way, you can have the dog sit to accept petting, and praise him when he behaves properly. You are focusing on praise and on modifying his behaviour by rewarding him when he acts appropriately. By being gentle and by supervising his interactions, you are showing him that there is no need to be afraid or defensive.

SEXUAL BEHAVIOUR

Dogs exhibit certain sexual behaviours that may have influenced your choice of male or female when you first purchased your Neapolitan Mastiff. To a certain extent, spaying/neutering will eliminate these behaviours, but if you are purchasing a dog that you wish to breed, you should be aware of what you will have to deal with throughout the dog's life.

Female dogs usually have two oestruses per year with each season lasting about three weeks. These are the only times in which a female dog will mate, and she usually will not allow this until the second week of the cycle, but this does vary from bitch to bitch.

If not bred during the heat cycle, it is not uncommon for a bitch to experience a false pregnancy, in which her mammary glands swell and she exhibits maternal tendencies toward toys or other objects.

Owners must further recognise that mounting is not merely a sexual expression but also one of dominance. Be consistent and persistent and you will find that you can 'move mounters.'

CHEWING

The national canine pastime is chewing! Every dog loves to sink his 'canines' into a tasty bone, but sometimes that bone is attached to his owner's hand! Dogs need to chew, to massage their gums, to make their new teeth feel better and to exercise their jaws. This is a natural behaviour deeply imbedded in all things canine. Our role as owners is not to stop the dog's chewing, but to redirect it to positive, chew-worthy objects. Be an informed owner and purchase proper chew toys like strong nylon bones that will not splinter. Be sure that the devices are safe and durable, since your dog's safety is at risk. Again, the owner is responsible for ensuring a dog-proof environment. The best answer is prevention: that is, put your shoes, handbags and other tasty objects in their proper places (out of the reach of the growing canine mouth). Direct puppies to their toys whenever you see them tasting the furniture legs or the leg of your trousers. Make a loud noise to attract the pup's attention and immediately escort him to his chew toy and engage him with the toy for at least four minutes, praising and encouraging him all the while.

Some trainers recommend deterrents, such as hot pepper or another bitter spice or a product designed for this purpose, to discourage the dog from chewing unwanted objects. Test these products yourself before investing in a large quantity.

JUMPING UP

Jumping up is a dog's friendly way of saying hello! Some dog owners do not mind when their dog jumps up, which is fine for them. The problem arises when guests come to the house and the dog greets them in the same manner—whether they like it or not! However friendly the greeting

> **Did You Know?**
>
> Dogs get to know each other by sniffing each other's backsides. It seems that each dog has a telltale odour probably created by the anal glands. It also distinguishes sex and signals when a female will be receptive to a male's attention.
> Some dogs snap at the other dog's intrusion of their private parts.

> **Did You Know?**
>
> When a dog bites there is always a good reason for it doing so. Many dogs are trained to protect a person, an area or an object. When that person, area or object is violated, the dog will attack. A dog attacks with its mouth. It has no other means of attack. It never uses teeth for defense. It merely runs away or lies down on the ground when it is in an indefensible situation. Fighting dogs (and there are many breeds which fight) are taught to fight, but they also have a natural instinct to fight. This instinct is normally reserved for other dogs, though unfortunate accidents occur when babies crawl towards a fighting dog and the dog mistakes the crawling child as a potential attacker.
> If a dog is a biter for no reason, if it bites the hand that feeds it or if it snaps at members of your family, see your veterinary surgeon or behaviourist immediately to learn how to modify the dog's behaviour.

may be, the chances are that your visitors will not appreciate your dog's enthusiasm. The dog will not be able to distinguish upon whom he can jump and whom he cannot. Therefore, it is probably best to discourage this behaviour entirely.

Pick a command such as 'Off' (avoid using 'Down' since you

will use that for the dog to lie down) and tell him 'Off' when he jumps up. Place him on the ground on all fours and have him sit, praising him the whole time. Always lavish him with praise and petting when he is in the sit position. That way you are still giving him a warm affectionate greeting, because you are as excited to see him as he is to see you!

DIGGING
Digging, which is seen as a destructive behaviour to humans, is actually quite a natural behaviour in dogs. Whether or not your dog is one of the 'earth dogs' (also known as terriers), his desire to dig can be irrepressible and most frustrating to his owners. When digging occurs in your garden, it is actually a normal behaviour redirected into something the dog can do in his everyday life. In the wild, a dog would be actively seeking food, making his own shelter, etc. He would be using his paws in a purposeful manner for his survival. Since you provide him with food and shelter, he has no need to use his paws for these purposes, and so the energy that he would be using may manifest itself in the form of little holes all over your garden and flower beds.

Perhaps your dog is digging as a reaction to boredom—it is somewhat similar to someone

eating a whole bag of crisps in front of the TV—because they are there and there is not anything better to do! Basically, the answer is to provide the dog with adequate play and exercise so that his mind and paws are occupied, and so that he feels as if he is doing something useful.

Of course, digging is easiest to control if it is stopped as soon as possible, but it is often hard to catch a dog in the act. If your dog is a compulsive digger and is not easily distracted by other activities, you can designate an area on your property where it is okay for him to dig. If you catch him digging in an off-limits area of the garden, immediately bring him to the approved area and praise him for digging there. Keep a close eye on him so that you can catch him in the act——that is the only way to make him understand what is permitted and what is not. If you take him to a hole he dug an hour ago and tell him 'No,' he will understand that you are not fond of holes, or dirt, or flowers. If you catch him whilst he is stifle-deep in your tulips, that is when he will get your message.

BARKING
Dogs cannot talk—oh, what they would say if they could! Instead, barking is a dog's way of 'talking.' It can be somewhat frustrating because it is not always easy to tell what a dog means by his

bark—is he excited, happy, frightened or angry? Whatever it is that the dog is trying to say, he should not be punished for barking. It is only when the barking becomes excessive, and when the excessive barking becomes a bad habit, that the behaviour needs to be modified. Fortunately, Neapolitan Mastiffs are not as vocal as most other dogs, and they tend to use their barks more purposefully than most dogs. If an intruder came into your home in the middle of the night and your Neapolitan Mastiff barked a warning, wouldn't you be pleased? You would probably deem your dog a hero, a wonderful guardian and protector of the home. Most dogs are not as discriminate as the Neapolitan Mastiff. For instance, if a friend drops by unexpectedly and rings the doorbell and is greeted with a sudden sharp bark, you would probably be annoyed at the dog. But in reality, isn't this just the same behaviour? The dog does not know any better...unless he sees who is at the door and it is someone he knows, he will bark as a means of vocalising that his (and your) territory is being threatened. Whilst your friend is not posing a threat, it is all the

A dam may act very protective of her pups. This is instinct and usually not the sign of an aggressive dog.

same to the dog. Barking is his means of letting you know that there is an intrusion, whether friend or foe, on your property. This type of barking is instinctive and should not be discouraged.

Excessive habitual barking, however, is a problem that should be corrected early on. As your Neapolitan Mastiff grows up, you will be able to tell when his barking is purposeful and when it is for no reason. You will become able to distinguish your dog's different barks and their meanings. For example, the bark when someone comes to the door will be different from the bark when he is excited to see you. It is similar to a person's tone of voice, except that the dog has to rely totally on tone of voice because he does not have the benefit of using words. An incessant barker will be evident at an early age.

There are some things that encourage a dog to bark. For example, if your dog barks non-stop for a few minutes and you give him a treat to quieten him, he believes that you are rewarding him for barking. He will associate barking with getting a treat, and will keep doing it until he is rewarded.

FOOD STEALING

Is your dog devising ways of stealing food from your coffee table? If so, you must answer the following questions: Is your Neapolitan Mastiff hungry, or is he 'constantly famished' like many dogs seem to be? Face it, some dogs are more food-motivated than others. Some dogs are totally obsessed by the smell of food and can only think of their next meal. Food stealing is terrific fun and always yields a great reward—FOOD, glorious food.

The owner's goal, therefore, is to be sensible about where food is placed in the home, and to reprimand the dog whenever he is caught in the act of stealing. But remember, only reprimand the dog if you actually see him stealing, not later when the crime is discovered for that will be of no use at all and will only serve to confuse.

BEGGING

Just like food stealing, begging is a favourite pastime of hungry puppies! It yields that same lovely reward—FOOD! Dogs quickly learn that their owners keep the 'good food' for themselves, and that we humans do not dine on dried food alone. Begging is a conditioned response related to a specific stimulus, time and place. The sounds of the kitchen, cans and bottles opening, crinkling bags, the smell of food in preparation, etc., will excite the dog and soon the paws are in the air!

Here is the solution to stopping this behaviour: Never give in to a beggar! You are rewarding the dog for sitting pretty, jumping up, whining and rubbing his nose into you by giving him that glorious reward—food. By ignoring the dog, you will (eventually) force the behaviour into extinction. Note that the behaviour likely gets worse before it disappears, so be sure there are not any 'softies' in the family who will give in to little 'Oliver' every time he whimpers, 'More, please.'

SEPARATION ANXIETY

Your Neapolitan Mastiff may howl, whine or otherwise vocalise his displeasure at your leaving the house and his being left alone. This is a normal reaction, no different from the child who cries as his mother leaves him on the first day at school. In fact, constant attention can lead to separation anxiety in the first place. If you are endlessly fussing over your dog, he will come to expect this from you all of the time and it will be more traumatic for him when you are not there. Obviously, you enjoy spending time with your dog, and he thrives on your love and attention. However, it should not become a dependent relationship where he is heartbroken without you.

One thing you can do to minimise separation anxiety is to make your entrances and exits as low-key as possible. Do not give your dog a long drawn-out goodbye, and do not overly lavish him with hugs and kisses when you return. This is giving in to the attention that he craves, and it will only make him miss it more when you are away. Another thing you can try is to give your dog a treat when you leave; this will not only keep him occupied and keep his mind off the fact that you have just left, but it will also help him associate your leaving with a pleasant experience.

You may have to accustom your dog to being left alone in intervals. Of course, when your dog starts whimpering as you approach the door, your first instinct will be to run to him and comfort him, but do not do it! Really—eventually he will adjust and be just fine if you take it in small steps. His anxiety stems from being placed in an unfamiliar situation; by familiarising him with being alone he will learn that he is okay. That is not to say you should purposely leave your dog home alone, but the dog needs to know that whilst he can depend on you for his care, you do not have to be by his side 24 hours a day.

When the dog is alone in the house, he should be confined to his designated dog-proof area of the house. This should be the area in which he sleeps and already feels comfortable so he will feel more at ease when he is alone.

My Neapolitan Mastiff

PUT YOUR PUPPY'S FIRST PICTURE HERE

Dog's Name _____ Strauss _____

Date _____ Photographer _____